JN074934

幼保 英語検定

Level
1 級 テ キ ス ト

【著者】 一般社団法人 幼児教育・保育英語検定協会

BOOKFORE
ブックフォレ　　株式会社ブックフォレ

目次

目次

目次

目次

＊テキスト音源は、こちらのホームページよりダウンロードをしてください。

HP　https://bookfore.co.jp/glh/download/

幼児教育・保育英語検定協会
（略称：幼保英語検定協会）

幼児教育、保育環境の国際的なグローバル化に対応できる幼稚園教諭及び保育士等幼児教育者養成の一環として、全国の幼稚園・保育園並びに幼稚園教諭・保育士養成学科を有する大学・短大及び専門学校と連携・協力して、幼保英語検定の実施を通し必要な実用的な英語の習得及び向上に資するため、英語の能力を判定し、またさまざまな活躍の機会を拡げその能力を養成することにより、日本の幼児教育、保育現場の向上に寄与することを目的としています。

また、諸外国における乳幼児教育分野の研究成果等を日本に紹介し、乳幼児教育分野の発展に寄与する活動にも積極的に取り組むことを目的とします。

幼児教育・保育英語検定
（略称：幼保英語検定）

特色

幼保英語検定は、幼稚園、こども園及び保育園等幼児教育施設において、英語でのコミュニケーション力の習得状況を知り、さらに向上させる機会となります。乳幼児との会話、園内の教育・保育に焦点をあて、現場に即した実用的な英語を習得できることが大きな特色です。

園内教育・保育及び保護者との日常会話から連絡・交流に必要な題材まで、受検者の学習を考慮し工夫した内容になっており、楽しみながら知識を深められる構成となっています。「入門レベル」から責任者として活躍できる「専門レベル」までの5段階で構成されており、英語力の向上が実感できます。資格を取得すると、幼児教育、保育分野で幅広く活用することができ、幼児教育、保育環境の国際的なグローバル化に対応できる実用的な英語を取得できます。

About Youho Eigo Kentei

Youho Eigo Kentei (Test of English for Early Childhood Educators) is designed for early childhood educators based on the daily routines and annual curriculum of Japanese preschools and kindergartens. This test is administered by Youho Eigo Kentei Kyokai (Organization of English for Early Childhood Educators). The test gives test takers a guideline to increase their language and comprehension levels, of both Japanese and English, by focusing on early childhood education, assessing reading, writing, listening, and speaking skills. We work closely with over 200 universities, colleges, technical schools, and high schools in Japan that have early childhood education departments. We also work with universities and Japanese schools overseas for non-native Japanese speakers who want to improve their professional skills. The test certificate shows that the person designated possesses the English proficiency level of the grade in which he or she has been certified.

本書について

本書は、幼保英語検定1級のテキストです。

本書は、「園児募集の章」から「園の運営管理の章」までの4つの章で、各章とも、職員同士、職員と保護者及び園外の方々との会話、各種文章作成と参考資料から構成されています。

この級に園児との会話はありません。

会話文は、職員同士、先生と保護者との会話から成り立っており、各会話は、左のページに日本語による会話を記載し、右のページに英訳を記載しています。
本書は、幼保英語検定1級級の能力目安に準拠し、幼保英語を使って高度なコミュニケーションと文書の作成が可能で、支障なく幼児教育現場での活動を行えるレベルの英語力の習得を目的としています。
幼保英語検定1級の目安は、大学上級程度です。

本書の特色
日本における保育、幼児教育現場に即した内容を前提としています。
園での日常活動で使われる英語や英語表現を身につけることができるよう工夫しており、紹介シーンも、日本の習慣や行事など、日本での保育、幼児教育を前提としています。
  ① 説明や解説の文章の中に記載している英語の表記には、「　」（カギカッコ）をつけています。「　」（カギカッコ）は日本語の文章の会話文を表記する方法として使われ、文中の英語には通常、""（クォーテーション）や斜体で区別しますが、「　」（カギカッコ）は区別が明確にしやすいため、本書では説明や解説の際に日本語及び英語のイディオムや単語の区分方法として採用しています。
  ② 人物の呼称は、英語圏では園児はファーストネームを使い、先生や保護者などにはMr.、Mrs.、Ms.をつけて使いますが、日本の生活慣習から違和感を生じないよう、英会話文でも、園児は「○○-kun、○○-chan」、先生は「○○-sensei」、保護者には「○○-san」と表現しています。
  ③ 会話文は日本文が一文でも、英文は2文に、またその逆になっている文もありますが、これは日本語、英語それぞれが自然な会話になるように作成したことによります。

なお、参考資料は、「文書作成例」、「工作資料」及び「実際のインターナショナルプリスクールで使用されている書類の一部（提供資料）」から構成されていますが、実務資料として掲載しているもので、検定出題対象ではありません。

本書を十分に学習され、早期に幼保英語検定1級に合格されることを祈念しております。

本書では、実際の園の会話を想定できるよう、バーチャルプリスクールを設定しています。

園名　　フォレガーデン園

所在地　　東京都港区麻布２丁目

最寄駅　　北東線麻布駅徒歩10分

避難場所　　有栖川山公園（通称アリス公園）

電話　　03－987－9876　　　　メール　　azabu2@ac.ko.jp

園の紹介　　0歳児より未就学児まで
乳児1歳児未満　　　10名
2歳児未満　　　　　15名
2歳児　　　　　　　15名
3歳児　　　　　　　20名
4歳児　　　　　　　20名
5歳児各　　　　　　30名

園の内容　　2階建て、保健室、園庭、プール、調理室、屋上広場あり

主な登場人物　　園長　　　　山田　　けいこ
（園長代行）　ポール　山田
事務長　　　梶山　　さとる
事務　　　　青山　　えりか
保育士1　　鈴木　　よしこ
保育士2　　勝　　　ゆうと
職員　　　　木村　　ゆか
新卒保育士1　南田　　まどか
新卒保育士2　村松　　まゆこ
園児　　　　荒木　　たえこ　　保護者
園児　　　　小野　　ひろし　　保護者

第1章　園児募集の章
Chapter 1　Student Recruitment Meeting

春は、桜の花のようにどの園も新しい園児の笑顔が満開になります。園児たちが安心してそして楽しんでもらえる園になるよう、先生たちは一生懸命です。年間行事予定の決定や入園希望の保護者向けの園の説明会や見学会の準備は、先生方にとっても大事な業務の一つです。

園児募集条件を決める

これから、来年度の園児募集の内容を決めたいと思います。募集人数は昨年と同数にしたいと思います。

複数の園に申し込むご家庭もいるので、今年は若干名多めに入園許可を出してはどうでしょうか？

覚えていらっしゃると思いますが、昨年、一昨年と２年連続して実際の入園者数が定員を割り込みました。

そうですね、覚えていますが、当園で入園手続きをされた園児が全員入園した場合、定員を超えてしまいます。ですから、やはり今までの人数で入園を許可をしましょう。

むしろ、お申し込みいただいた保護者の方々に当園の良さをこれまで以上にお話をすることで、当園に、納得してお子様たちを通わせていただけるようにしましょう。

そうですね。園に来て見学していただくと当園の良さが分かっていただけますし、入園させたいと思っていただけると思います。

今年は、保護者向けの説明会を少し早めにやってはどうでしょうか？

もしくは、見学会の回数も増やしてはどうでしょうか？

そうですね。両方ともいいアイディアですね！早速検討しましょう。

それと、今年のパンフレットには、多くの園児や保護者の写真を載せるように考えてみましょう。

木村先生、保護者の方に園のパンフレットへの写真利用の了解を取っていただけますか？

分かりました。パンフレットが、７月には出来上がるよう準備します。

では、青山先生、決裁書を作成し終わったら、すぐに園長室まで持ってきてください。なお、印刷の予算は、できるだけ抑えて立ててください。

パンフレットに、園児や保護者の方の写真を載せるとなると従来のA4の2つ折りサイズからB4サイズに変更してスペースを新たにもうけなければいけません。また、コート紙から光沢紙に変える必要もあります。予算がかなり増加しますが、そこは、印刷の時間を昨年よりできるだけ長くして、印刷費を抑えてもらうようにします。

Deciding on Criteria for Student Recruitment

 I would like to discuss next year's student recruitment. I'm thinking about setting the same quota as last year for the number of children we will accept.

 Some families apply to several schools at the same time, so wouldn't it be a good idea to accept a few extra students this year?

If you remember, the number of students who have enrolled has fallen below the target for the last two years.

 Yes, I remember, but if everyone who applies to our school is accepted and decides to enroll their children, then the number of students would exceed our capacity. So, it's better if we only accept our established quota when enrolling new students.

Instead, we should try to better communicate the positive points of our school to any parents who apply, so that they will be convinced to enroll their daughter or son here.

 I agree. Once they come and have a look, I am sure they will see all the great things we are doing here and will want their children to join.

 What if we have our Parent's Information Day a bit earlier this year?

 Or, perhaps we could offer Open House visits more frequently?

 Yes. Both of these ideas sound great! We'll take them into account right away.

Also, let's see if we can try to get more student and parent pictures for our brochure this year.

Kimura-sensei, can you ask the parents for permission to use their and their children's photographs in our brochure?

 Sure. I'll try to get the brochures ready by July.

 Aoyama-sensei, please prepare the approval form and bring it to my office as soon as possible. Also, please try to keep the printing budget as low as possible.

 If we are to add the children's and parents' pictures to the brochure, we may need to change the size of the layout—from an A4 sheet of paper folded in half to the larger B4 to add extra space. We should also switch from matte to glossy paper. Doing this will likely make costs go up drastically, but we can make up for it by allowing more time for printing than last year.

外国人の子どもの入園

来年の園児募集の件で他に議題がありますか？

市から連絡があり、来年、外国人のお子さんの受け入れの打診が来ていますが。

何人ほどと言っていましたか？

現段階では、3名いて、5歳のモハメドくん、4歳のジェシカちゃんと2歳のスジンちゃんです。3人のお子さんとご家族について市から参考資料を受け取っています。これがその資料です。

なるほど…。どの子も、日本に来てあまり日が経っていませんね。ご家族は日本語がどの程度できるのですか？

現時点でご家族は、日本語は少ししかお話しにならないようです。諸連絡の際には英語が中心になると思います。

そうでしょうね。当園としてはこの3名については受け入れたいと思います。

様々な国の園児が入ってきてくれることは、楽しみですね。

身近なところで文化の違いを感じられていい刺激になっています。園児たちも私たち職員も多くの新しいことや大切なことを学ぶと思います！

当園に入園を希望される保護者の方には、当園が外国のお子様を受け入れることに熱心なことをご理解いただけるといいですね。

保護者の方も文化を超えてコミュニケーションをとっていただく様子も見たいですね。

この園の子どもたちが肌で異文化を学び理解をする、まさに草の根交流ですね。

広がっていくと良いですね。

Enrolling International Students

What other items on the agenda do we have regarding the requirements for next year's student recruitment?

City hall has contacted us and would like us to accept international students as well next year.

Did they say approximately how many students there might be?

At this time there are three students, Muhammad, age 5, Jessica, age 4, and Sue-Jin, age 2. We received reference materials from the city hall about these children and their families. Here are the files.

I see⋯None of these children have been in Japan for very long. How much Japanese do the family members speak?

At this point, most of the family members speak very little Japanese. I think English will be their main medium of communication at our school.

I agree. I'd like to welcome these three students to our school.

It's definitely exciting to have students from different countries join our school community.

I think it's very stimulating to experience cultural diversity around us. I believe our students and staff members will learn many new and important things!

It would be great if the parents who want to enroll their children here recognize our enthusiasm in accepting international students.

It will also be interesting to see the parents communicating across cultural boundaries.

That is precisely an example of the type of grassroots exchange we need to help our children here learn to live with, and to understand, people from different countries.

It'll be great to see this catch on.

フォレガーデン入園案内 （要約）

園の見学

園のウェブサイトに記載の毎週金曜日のキャンパスツアー・インフォメーションセッションもしくは、毎月最終土曜日に開催されるオープンハウスに園見学を行ってください。

募集対象児

1歳児　16人（2クラス・各8人）　　　2歳児　20人（2クラス・各10人）
3歳児　16人　　　　　4歳児　18人　　　　　5歳児　18人
クラス分けは、9月1日時点の年齢によって決定します。

入園資格・入園優先基準

基礎的な園での生活ができる程度に身体的・精神的に成熟していること
以下の優先順位により受け入れます：
- ◆ 在園児
- ◆ 兄弟姉妹
- ◆ 外国のパスポートを持つ子ども
- ◆ 他のインターナショナルスクールからの転園する子ども
- ◆ その他

出願と入園手続き

- 願書は園のウェブサイトより10月1日よりダウンロードできます。
- 願書は10月15日より郵送、ファックス、またはEメールの添付ファイルで願書手数料と一緒に提出が可能です。
- 書類選考を行ったのち、通過者は11月に入園試験を行います
- 結果通知は、1月の第2金曜日までに通知します。

保育料

入園料：	108,000円（1回のみ・返金不可）	
第1期 （8月から12月）	第2期 （1月から3月）	第3期 （4月から6月）
378,000 円	324,000 円	378,000 円
料金はすべて税込みです。		

Fore Garden Preschool
A Guide to Entering Preschool

Visitations

You may schedule a visit to the school through the website by joining our "Campus Tour & Information Sessions" events held every Friday, or "Open House" events held the last Saturday of each month.

Availability

Year 1 Classes   16 seats (2 classes, 8 seats each)
Year 2 Classes   20 seats (2 classes, 10 seats each)
Year 3 Class   16 seats
Year 4 Class   18 seats
Year 5 Class   18 seats

Class placement is determined by the child's age on September 1st of that school year

Eligibility, Admissions Priorities

Students must meet a basic level of age-appropriate readiness with regards to physical, emotional and social maturity.
Students are accepted according to the following priorities:
- Currently enrolled, continuing students
- Siblings
- Students with a foreign passport
- Students transferring from another international school
- All others

Application Procedures

- You may download the application form from the school website from October 1st
- Application form may be submitted from October 15th by post, fax or email attachment along with the application fee (see below)
- The school will review all applications and contact eligible applicants for a screening test in November
- Everyone will be informed of their results by the second Friday in January

Tuition

Registration:	108,000 yen (one-time, non-refundable fee)	
Term 1 (August to December)	Term 2 (January to March)	Term 3 (April to June)
378,000 yen	324,000 yen	378,000 yen
Please note that all figures include tax		

入園手続き （要約）

当園の入園願書手続きの流れ：

● キャンパスツアー・インフォメーションセッションもしくはオープンハウスに参加の上、園見学にお越しください。

　園見学の日程は、当園のウェブサイトを参照してください。

● 郵便、ファックス、または E メールの添付ファイルで以下の書類を園に提出してください。

　　　◆ 願書（ウェブサイトより入手可能）

　　　◆ 健康記録と家庭調査票

　　　◆ 住民票（原本ではなくコピーを提出してください）

　　　◆ 子どもの写真、家族の写真（各1枚提出してください）

　　　◆ 奨学金申請書と前年度の申告書（該当する場合）

　　　◆ 前園からの書類（該当する場合のみ）

● 書類通過者は、入学審査が行われます。

● 入園許可された場合、入園許可書および入園の際の諸費用の請求書が送られる。期日までお支払いがない場合は、入園できない場合がありますのでご注意ください。（補欠の方への連絡をいたします）

● 保護者手引書と園の資料をお渡しします。当園の必要事項が記載されています。（カレンダー、準備するもの、保育方針）

● 入園初日に、園規定シャツ、帽子、かばんをお渡しします。

Fore Garden Application

These steps will guide you through our school's application process.

- Please arrange a school visit through a Campus Tour & Information Session or Open House.

  Please see our website for a list of upcoming opportunities to visit and to register.

- Submit the following documents to the school by post, fax, or email attachment:

    ◆ Application Form（available through our website）

    ◆ Health & Family Questionnaire Form

    ◆ Residential Registration Form（please submit a copy and not the original）

    ◆ A clear photograph of the student and his or her family（two separate photos, please）

    ◆ Scholarship Application Form and Tax Returns from Previous Year
       （if applicable）

    ◆ Reports from previous school（if available）

- Eligible applicants will be invited to a screening session.

- The families of children who are accepted will receive a letter of acceptance and an invoice for all fees. Those who do not pay by the deadline may lose their seat to the next available candidate.

- You will receive an information packet from the school with a copy of our Parent Handbook. This contains all the information you need to join the school（calendar, things to prepare, policy explanation）.

- Children will receive a school shirt, hat, and bag on the first day they attend school.

フォレガーデン園 入園試験における年齢別発達度目安（4歳児）(要約)

本園は以下の基準に従い、入園試験にてお子さまを評価します。
これらの基準は、基本的な子どもの発達基準を元に作成されました。

学習への取り組み

自発性（好奇心、自己方向性を示す）

関心・意欲（問題解決への意欲と努力を示す）

社会的・情緒的発達

関係構築（先生や友だちとよい人間関係を築く）

情緒的安定（集中力・感情を抑制する力）

身体発達

運動能力（走る・ジャンプする・バランス能力）

手先の力（鉛筆をしっかりと握る・ハサミで切る）

言語・読み書き能力

アルファベットの知識（すべての大文字・一部の小文字を理解している）

フォニックス（文字と音を結びつける・20以上のサイトワードが読める）

算数

数える（12まで数えて理解できる）

並べ替える（サイズ・色・カテゴリごとに並べ替えることができる）

表現力

芸術的理解（絵を描くことなど、何かを表現するために材料を使う）

音楽的能力（英語で歌を歌い、基本的なリズムをとる）

物事の認知能力

観察力（5感を使い観察し、表現できる）

推測力（観察と知識をもとに結果を推測することができる）

Fore Garden Student Screening Guidelines (Year 4)

During the screening process, the school will evaluate your child according to these criteria.

These guidelines were created using basic child developmental standards.

Approaches to Learning
Initiative (shows curiosity, self-direction)
Engagement (shows willingness and effort towards problem solving)

Social and Emotional Development
Relationship Building (interacts appropriately with teachers and peers)
Emotional Stability (reasonable concentration, controls feelings)

Physical Development
Athletic Ability (runs, uns, jumps, balances, moves with confidence)
Fine Motor Skills (hold pencil properly, cuts with scissors)

Language and Literacy
Alphabetical Knowledge (knows all uppercase letters, some lowercase)
Phonics (can connect some letters to sounds, reads 20 sight words or more)

Mathematics
Counting (can count and understand up to number 12)
Sorting (can sort objects by category – size, color, etc.)

Creative Arts
Artistic Understanding (uses materials to represent something, such as drawing pictures)
Musical Ability (Sings song in English and follows basic rhythm)

Science and Technology
Observation (uses the five senses to observe and express characteristics)
Guesswork (uses observation and knowledge to guess outcomes)

パンフレットを作る

急いで来年度の園児募集のパンフレット作りに取り掛からないといけないわ。印刷屋さんに連絡して、打ち合わせを始めないといけないですね。

いつもの印刷屋さんですね？いくつかの業者から見積もりを出してもらいますか？

いえ、当園のことをよくわかっているし、今年も使用できるデータも持っているから、いつもの印刷屋さんにお願いしましょう。

わかりました、今からお電話してみます。打ち合わせはいつにしますか？先生のご都合のよい日時をいくつか出していただけたら、予定を調整します。

わかりました。今週はスケジュールが立て込んでいるから、来週の水曜、金曜の17時以降か土曜日の午前中で決めてもらえますか？

分かりました。すぐに連絡します。私も打ち合わせに同席した方がよいですか？それと、打ち合わせまでに準備しておくものがありますか？

そうですね・・・パンフレットの内容とホームページの内容は一緒でないと困りますから、パンフレットの内容が決まったら、ホームページも変更しなければいけませんね。予め、インターネット業者の方にも連絡しておいてもらえますか？

分かりました、今日のうちにメールをしておきます。インターネット業者の担当者のお名前とメールアドレスを教えてもらえますか？

もちろん、午後に転送しておきます。

Making Brochures

I need to begin working on the brochures for next year's student recruitment as soon as possible. I guess I should contact the printing company and set up a meeting with them.

It's the same printing company we usually use, right? Should we contact some different companies to get a list of quotes?

No, let's just stick with our usual place, because they know us really well, and they already have some data that we can use again for this year's brochure.

Okay, I'll contact them right away. When do you want to arrange the meeting? If you could tell me which dates and times you're available, I'll arrange the appointment.

Alright. I'm pretty busy this week, so can you set up a meeting for either Wednesday or Friday next week, after 5 p.m., or Saturday morning?

I got it. I'll contact them immediately. Would it be better if I join you at the meeting? Also, is there anything you would like me to do prepare for the meeting?

Let's see⋯ The contents for both the brochure and the website should be exactly the same. So, once we decide what we want to put in the brochure, we should also make those changes to the website. Could you please make sure to contact the internet company as well?

Okay, I'll email them today. Can you tell me the name and email address of the person in charge at the internet company?

Sure, I'll forward you the information later this afternoon.

業者を呼ぶ

おはようございます。今年のフォレガーデン園のパンフレットの件でご連絡しております。今年は早めにパンフレットを完成させたいので、今回の期日までに間に合うように、よろしくお願いします。

いつもお引き立て賜わり、ありがとうございます。ご希望の予定に合わせて印刷を終わらせるよう努力させていただきます。ご希望の期限を教えていただけますか？

はい、できれば7月には配布を始めたいのですが。

分かりました。あまりのんびりできないですね。パンフレットのレイアウトやページ数はすでに決まっていますか？

はい、B4サイズの用紙を2つ折り、4ページでお願いします。1ページ目は表紙、開いた左ページに園長のご挨拶を入れてください。そして、右のページに園の1年の園活動の紹介、裏のページに1日の園の生活を入れたいのですが。

書式やフォントは昨年のパンフレットで使用したものと同一でよろしいですか？

保護者だけでなく、お子様にも読んでいただきたいので、もっと楽しい感じの文字にしていただけますか？あともう一つ大きな文字でお願いできますか？最後に、ひらがなで漢字にルビを打っていただけますか？

わかりました、できます。あと、新しいパンフレットに掲載するお子様たちの写真や資料はいつごろ頂けますか？

今、保護者の方々の掲載の承諾を取っていますから、来週後半には必要なものすべてお渡しできると思います。

お渡しはデータでよいですか？

はい、もちろんです。データが重いようでしたら、データ便で送ってください。なお、PDF では送らないでくださいね、時々わかりづらい場合がありますから。

Contacting a Printing Company

Hello. Good morning. I am calling to make arrangements for this year's new Fore Garden Preschool brochures. I'd like to complete the brochure earlier than last year, and we would appreciate your help in meeting this new deadline.

Thank you for your continued business with us. We will try our best to finish the printing according to your new schedule. Can you please tell me your preferred deadline?

Yes, I'd like to start distributing the brochures in July if possible.

I understand. Then, we don't have much time. Have you already decided the layout and the number of pages for the brochure?

Yes, we would like a two-fold brochure with 4 pages on B4 paper. The first page will be the front cover, and once you open the brochure, on the left side there will be a message from the principal. Then, on the right side, we would like to include an introduction to the year's activities at the school, and on the back, we would like to include the daily schedule.

Would you like to use the same style and font that you used for last year's brochure?

Since we'd like to have both the parents and children read the brochure, we were wondering if it is possible to change the font to something more playful? Also, we'd like the font to be one size bigger. Lastly, is it possible for you to also add the hiragana reading over the kanji?

Yes, we can do that. Also, when can you provide us with the pictures of the children and the information that you'd like to include in the new brochure?

We're contacting the parents for permission right now, so I think we'll be able to provide everything you need by the end of next week.

Can I give them to you as a data file?

Yes, of course. But if the file is too heavy, please use a file transfer service. Also, please don't send the data as a PDF file, because sometimes it is hard to read.

パンフレットづくり（印刷物）の基礎知識
2つ折りのパンフレット作り

パンフレットを作るときは、ページごとにテーマを決めて、全体の構成を考えます。しかし、ページの構成にはちょっとした注意が必要です。例をあげて説明しましょう。

図①：2枚の二つ折りにした紙を重ねます。
ここでは、二つ折りにしたⒶの紙に、二つ折りしたⒷの紙を差し込んでいます。紙Ⓐの外側は、パンフレットの表表紙と裏表紙になります。ページは、表紙を除くと全部で6ページになります。
ページの構成は、⒜の表表紙の裏が1ページ目となり、これに向き合う⒝の面が2ページ目、開いた次が3ページ目、4ページ目となり、⒝面の最後が5ページ目、5ページ目と向き合う⒜の裏表紙の裏面が6ページとなります。
しかし、ページ番号を打ってばらばらにして開いてみると分かりますが、隣り合ったページの番号が違います。これらを間違えてしまうと、ページ構成がばらばらになってしまいます。

図②：また、用紙には印刷できる範囲が決まっています。印刷屋さんでは、印刷できる範囲を「トンボ」という角々の線で囲っています。この枠を超えた部分に書いたり貼ったりした文章や内容は切れてしまい印刷できません。

図①（Figure ①）

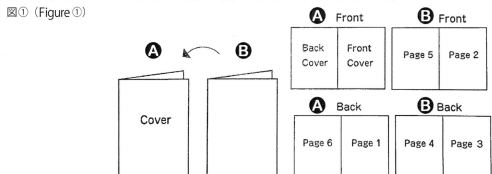

参考：その他の折り方

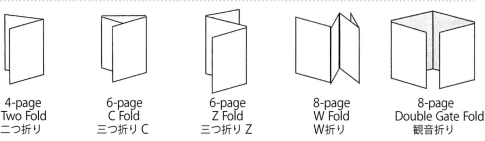

| 4-page
Two Fold
二つ折り | 6-page
C Fold
三つ折り C | 6-page
Z Fold
三つ折り Z | 8-page
W Fold
W折り | 8-page
Double Gate Fold
観音折り |

Let's Try ①

Basic Knowledge for Brochures / Printed Matters
Create a Two-Fold Brochure

When you make a brochure, be sure to set a theme for each page and build a framework for the page layout. There are a several points to consider very carefully. The following are some examples:

Figure ① Collate two pieces of papers, folded in half (Ⓐ and Ⓑ) .

In Figure 1, we insert paper Ⓑ into paper Ⓐ Paper Ⓐwill be the front and back cover of the brochure, so there will be six pages, not including the cover pages.

The back of the front cover page will be page 1 and the next page will be page 2. Then, if you flip the page, there will be pages 3 and 4. After that, page 5 will be the last page of paper Ⓑ. The back cover of Ⓐ facing the 5th page will be page 6.

If you number each of the pages, you will notice that the pages adjacent to each printed page will not be in the order that you will see when you open the brochure. Please be aware if you make a mistake in numbering the pages, you will have trouble making brochure layout.

Figure ② Please also understand that there is a limit to the print area. Printers usually set the print area by indicating crop or trim marks. If you type or paste copied text or images outside this area, then it won t' appear on the page when it gets printed.

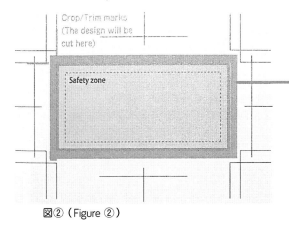

図②（Figure ②）

3mm bleed area	ヌリダシ
This area will be trimmed away. Extend the background into the bleed area when your design goes to the edge of the page	ヌリダシとは裁断用に3mm あける部分を指します。ここの部分は裁断します。ページの端（余白なし）をデザインする時は、裁断する場所を確保できるようにします。

BC

来年度の行事予定の会議1

本日は来年度の行事の予定を話し合います。

今年の有栖川山公園への遠足は、保護者の皆さんに好評でした。有栖川山公園は、災害時の指定避難場所にもなっているので、道順を覚える良い機会にもなっていました。

それはよかったです。今年はその部分を強調して、もっと多くの保護者の方の参加も呼びかけてみましょう。

あと、来年の夏は猛暑が予想されているので、プール開きの予定を早めるのはいかがですか?

それもいいですが、夏にサマータイムを導入することになっているので、7月からの登園時間を30分早めてはどうでしょうか?

登園時間を30分早めると、降園時間が早くなって、困る保護者がでますね。

そうですね、ヨーロッパや北アメリカのように時計を夏時間にしてくれたらよいのですが。

先生方の負担は増えますが、7月〜9月の保育開始時間を30分早める延長保育としてもらってはどうでしょう。

大変そうですけど、園児の健康を考えると、先生方は協力してくれると思います。

そう思いますか?そうなると、先生方の就労時間の変更が必要になりますか?

本来ですと、先生方のシフトの変更が必要になりますが、期間が限定的です。早朝勤務手当の対象として対応していただいてはどうでしょうか?

そうですね。先生方の毎日の生活リズムに影響させたくないので、シフトの変更は、できるだけ避けるようにしてください。一番通園バスのお迎えや園の朝の準備は、私や青山先生がお手伝いしないといけませんね。

Meeting for Next Year's Event Schedule 1

Today, we're going to talk about next year's event schedule.

This year's excursion to Arisugawayama Park was a hit with all the parents. Arisugawayama Park is a designated evacuation site in the event of an emergency, so it was a great opportunity for everyone to remember the route there.

That's good to know. Let's emphasize that point this year and appeal to a larger group of parents to participate.

Also, the weather is expected to be extremely hot next summer, so what do you think about opening the pool early?

That could be an option, but since we'll be introducing a summer time shift during the summer, what if we move the arrival time to 30 minutes earlier starting in July?

If we start 30 minutes earlier, then the students would have to leave earlier and I'm pretty sure some parents won't be happy about that.

I see… I wish we had daylight savings here like they do in Europe and North America.

It'll be a heavier load for teachers, but why don't we start 30 minutes earlier and extend our school hours from July to September.

That'll be more work for us, but if we think about the students' health, I'm sure all teachers will be eager to cooperate.

You think so? If that's the case, do we need to change the working hours for the teachers?

Normally, we would need to change the teachers' shifts. However, since it's only for a limited amount of time, we could treat this "early bird shift" as over-time. What do you think?

You're right. If possible, please try to avoid changing the shifts, because we don't want to affect the teachers' daily routines. You and I should help out by greeting the students who arrive on the first bus and by taking care of the morning preparations.

来年度の行事予定の会議２

鈴木先生、来年度の行事予定の作成担当をやってもらえますか？

はい、喜んで。今年で５年目ですので、大体の流れも分かってきましたので。今年の行事に準じて予定をたてればよろしいのですよね？

はい。ただ、今年の引き取り訓練や避難訓練はもっと関連を持たせるようにしましょう。先日の大震災を踏まえて、火災訓練よりも地震を想定して行うのはどうでしょうか。

分かりました。それともう一つ提案があります。来年の発表会の演目として、園児による英語劇をやってもいいでしょうか？

それは素敵ですね。

実習に来る保育科の先生方にも協力していただいたらどうでしょうか？

それはいいアイディアね！たしかに英語による保育の科目に力を入れていますし、学内に英文科もありますし、助かりますよね。

早速、学科長に相談してみましょうね。きっと喜んで協力してくれますよ！

英語劇に使えるような物語がありますか？

はい、あります。「星座になったクマさん」という森に住む動物たちが災害に見舞われた時の思いやりを描いた物語です。

あ、あれね！私もその物語を知っているわ。ぴったりですね！

楽しみだわ！ぜひ、ご近所の方にも劇を見に来ていただきたいですね。

Meeting for Next Year's Event Schedule 2

Suzuki-sensei, do you think you could be in charge of coming up with next year's event schedule?

Sure, I'd love to. It'll be my fifth year, so I generally know how it works. Is it okay if I base it on this year's events?

Yes, for this year's emergency pick-up and evacuation drill, let's create a more relevant scenario. How about, rather than practicing a fire drill, we have an earthquake scenario, considering that there was a big earthquake recently.

Okay, sure. I have another suggestion as well. May I prepare a children's play in English for next year's school play?

That would be wonderful.

What if we ask the teachers from the Childcare Department, who come for practical training, to help out?

What a great idea! Their school focuses on subjects that teach childcare in English, and they even have an English department, so they would be a great help.

I'll speak with the head of the Childcare Department at once. I'm sure she'll be happy to cooperate!

Do you have a play in mind that's suitable for the children to do in English?

Yes, I have an idea. The story is called "Bears Who Become Stars" and it's about animals in the forest and how they care about one another during a time of a crisis.

Oh yes! I know that story too. It's just perfect! I'm very excited about this!

It'll be great to have our neighbors come and see the play as well.

説明会の準備

来週の週末に行う園の説明会の準備は大丈夫ですか？

はい、準備万端です。ご近所の方々には、来週の週末は交通渋滞や説明会の実施によってご不便や、ご迷惑をおかけする事もご連絡いたしました。あと、当日来園された方々に見ていただく、園の紹介ビデオも届いています。

それは良かったわ！当園の保護者の方々には、連絡帳に案内を挟んでお渡しして、興味のありそうなお知り合いの方をこの週末にお誘いいただくようにお願いしています。

当日は保護者の方向けのプレゼンテーションを午前に1回、午後に1回行うことにしています。やることがいっぱいですね。山田園長先生、プレゼンテーションの際に、お手伝いいただけるようよろしくお願いします。

はい、もちろんです、喜んで。プレゼンテーションでは、当園のことと園で行われていることをよく知ってもらわないといけませんからね。

園長先生のご挨拶のあとの園の紹介では、1年の園生活をまとめた DVD をご覧いただくことにしています。また、在籍園児の保護者の方数名にもフォレガーデン園での経験談をお話ししていただくようにお願いしています。

同伴される子どもたちの臨時お預かりの方はどうですか？

はい、準備は整えてありますので、大丈夫だと思います。試し保育となりますので、保健所には一時的収容数の増数の届け出もしました。当日オフの職員4名と補助職員3名の方にも休み返上で出勤していただけるように頼みました。

そうですか。それを聞いて安心しました。たくさんの方に来ていただけることを祈りましょう。当日は天気がよいようです。

Preparation for the Open House

How is the preparation for next weekend's Open House coming along?

It looks like we're ready to go. I've contacted the people living near the school to apologize in advance for the increase in traffic into the school over the weekend, and for any trouble our Open House event might cause. Also, we got the introduction video that we'll be showing to the visitors during our information session about the school.

That's great! I left a notice about this upcoming event in the communication book for parents. Also, I asked them to invite people they know who might be interested in joining this weekend.

We plan on having two presentations for the parents, one in the morning, and then another in the afternoon. It's going to be a lot of work. Yamada-encho, if you could help us out during the presentations, that would be great.

Yes, of course, I am happy to do so. I'd like the parents to know as much as possible about our school and learn more about what we do here through the presentations.

After Encho-sensei's greeting, we'll be playing a DVD showing all about the daily life of the school throughout the year. Also, we've asked some of our current parents to talk about their experiences at Fore Garden Preschool.

What about the temporary drop-off service for any children accompanying their parents?

Yes, we have taken care of this, so it should be alright. I notified the health care center in childcare about increasing the capacity temporarily as a trial session. I also asked four staff members and three back-up staff members, who normally have that day-off, to come in to work.

I see. I'm glad to hear that. Hopefully, we will have a lot of visitors at the Open House. Weather will be nice on that day.

保護者へのプレゼンテーション

本日は、フォレガーデン園にお越しいただきありがとうございます。

ただいまより、当園のご説明をさせていただきます。小さなお子様をお連れの保護者の方のために、本日は別室にて、お子様のお預かりを致しております。ご希望の方は、スタッフまでお申し出ください。では、園長よりご挨拶申し上げます。

本日は、ご多忙の中、当園にお越しいただきありがとうございます。私は、園長の山田でございます。フォレガーデン園にご来園いただきましたことをとても嬉しく思っております。

当園は、皆様の大切なお子様の健やかな成長のお手伝いができる安全と安心の施設と職員環境を備えております。当園では、お子様の体力作りに心がけており、屋外でのラジオ体操や縄跳び、鉄棒等屋外での運動を行っています。一方で、知育発達に欠かせない、指先を使った工作やアートを取り入れております。

バランスのとれた体力、知力、創造力となるように、当園では、健全な発育を促しています。また、地域で一番早くから幼児の段階で英語教育を取り入れ、その一環として、来日された外国人のお子様も受け入れております。幼少の頃から身近な国際性を修得できる国際的な環境を提供できるよう努めております。ぜひ、当園へのご入園を検討していただきますようお願い申し上げます。簡単ですが、挨拶とさせていただきます。

園長、ありがとうございました。では、私から園についてご説明をさせていただきます。はじめに、当園の1年間の様子を DVD でご覧いただきます。DVDは約10分ほどです。その後、当園にお子様をお預けになっている保護者の方2名にお子様を当園に入れることを決めたことに関してどう感じているか等をお話しいただくことになっております。園を選択される際のご参考にもなると思いますので、よろしくお願いします。

Open House - Presentation for the Parents

 Thank you for coming to Fore Garden Preschool today.

We would now like to begin the information session about our school. We are providing a drop-off service in the daycare room today for parents who have brought small children with them. If you wish to use the service, please inform one of our staff members. Now, a few words from Encho-sensei.

 Thank you for taking time out of your busy schedule today to attend our Open House. I am Yamada-encho and it is my pleasure to welcome you to Fore Garden Preschool.

Our school provides a safe and welcoming environment, with facilities and qualified staff to help your children to develop and grow. On one hand, we incorporate outdoor physical exercises to keep your children in good shape, such as our daily radio exercises, jump rope, or chin-up bars. On the other hand, we engage the children in many arts and crafts activities to help develop their fine motor skills, which are essential for their intellectual growth.

By equally valuing the physical, intellectual, and creative aspects of your child's learning, we can nurture his or her holistic development. We are the first school to incorporate an English education at the preschool level, and in doing so, we have accepted international students from abroad. We will work hard to provide an international environment where all our children can interact with each other in a multicultural way. Please consider enrolling your children here at our school. Thank you for listening.

 Thank you, Yamada-encho. Now, I would like to show you more about our school. Please take a look at this DVD that we have made to show you what a year at our school is like. The DVD will run approximately ten minutes. After the DVD, I have asked two of our current parents to come up and talk about how they feel about their decision to enroll their child here, and so on. I think this information can be used as a reference for other parents when selecting a preschool.

園長先生の挨拶（要約）

保護者各位

当園フォレガーデン園にご興味をいただきましてありがとうございます。当園は、皆様の大切なお子様が心身ともに健やかに成長できるよう、最高の環境を整えております。当園にご入園いただけることを大変うれしく思います。

当園では、お子様が望ましい成長ができるように様々な活動を取り入れております。お子様は、登園の体系的な活動と自由な活動を通しての学びを楽しむことができます。これは成長に必要な知識や能力を身につけるだけでなく、学んだことを自ら活用できる機会を設けるためです。お子様は教室で様々な活動や教材を使って過ごしたり、屋外での十分な時間を確保することで、自然やお友だちとの関わりを通して、園生活を存分に楽しむことができます。

また、様々な道具や材料の使い方を学び、様々な環境に社会的に適応する力も身につけていきます。先生からの質問にどう答えるかだけでなく、自分の持っている知識や能力をもとに、自分なりの答えを見つけることができるよう援助しています。

当園のすべてのカリキュラムと基準は、お子様の発達に関する最新の研究と、お子様の成長過程の理解に基づいています。乳幼児期はお子様の成長にとても大切な時期であり、精神的・身体的能力にはかなりの違いがあります。これらのことを踏まえ、これまでの経験と知識を基に、お子様に最も適した環境を提供できるよう努めています。

皆様に当園に来ていただけることを楽しみにしております。

私どもは、お子様の無限の可能性を信じ、楽しく過ごせるように努めてまいります。

Principal's Message from Fore Garden

Dear Parents,

Greetings and thank you for your interest in Fore Garden Preschool. Here at Fore Garden, we strive to create the best atmosphere for young children and their families, in order ensure that they can grow in body and mind in the best way possible. We are delighted that you are considering becoming a part of our community.

Students at Fore Garden enjoy a mix of activities that are designed to stimulate their development in a positive direction. Children enjoy both structured and unstructured learning time. This is so that they have time to acquire the knowledge and skills they need, but also the opportunity to use them in a self-directed manner. Students will be able to truly enjoy their school life by spending time in the classroom with a variety of activities and materials, and also by ensuring them a healthy amount of time outdoors to interact with nature and their peers.

Students are taught how to use different tools, interact with different materials, and also how to adapt socially to various environments. We teach students not only how to answer questions posed by teachers, but also how to ask their own questions and seek their answers with the skills available to them.

All the curriculum and standards of Fore Garden is based on the latest research into child development, and a strong understanding of how children develop over time. Each year in a young childs'life is critical for their growth and differs significantly in their mental and physical abilities. We take all this into account, along with our own experience and knowledge in order to create an environment that is most suitable for our students.

We thank you and sincerely hope to have the opportunity to welcome your family to Fore Garden International Preschool in the Future. Doing so will ensure your child a happy and positive future with limitless possibilities.

新年度を迎えるにあたり（要約）

フォレガーデン園での心躍るような新たな一年へようこそ。

在園児・新入園児の皆さまをお迎えするのをとてもうれしく思います。在園児の皆様には、温かい笑顔で新入園児の皆様をお迎えいただきたいと思います。

わからないことがあればお気軽にご連絡ください。わからないことは、担任の先生に直接質問していただくか、連絡帳に記入していただくようお願いいたします。また、私もご相談にのりますので、どんな些細なことでもいつでもお気軽にお尋ねください。

お子様やご家族の皆様が少しでもはやく園の生活に慣れていただけるように、イベントをご用意しております。

8月24日　　新入園児オリエンテーション
午前10時より新入園児向けのオリエンテーションを実施します。新入園のお子様は、保護者の方と一緒にご参加ください。このオリエンテーションは、お子様の担任の先生の紹介やクラスについてのお話などがあり、お子様の紹介もあります。また、当園の詳細やいくつかの注意事項を説明いたします。お昼ごろに終了いたします。

8月27日　　説明会
新入園ならびに在園、全てのお子様は、保護者の方とご一緒にご参加ください。午前10時より2時間を予定しています。

各クラスそれぞれ音楽・美術・読み聞かせなどを通して、お互い親しめる活動を考えております。そのあと、各クラスで昼食をとっていただいて、午後1時に解散になります。

当日は、給食がご利用いただけませんので、お弁当をお持ちください。

8月28日　　入園初日
新しいクラスで初日が始まります。新しいクラスは、お子様にとって大きな一歩であり、いつもと違う状況に戸惑いを感じることもありますので、保護者の方はたくさんの愛情を注いであげてください。園の生活に慣れるまで3週間ほどかかります。何かありましたら、いつでも担任や園長にご相談ください。

Welcome to Fore Garden Preschool and the New School Year!

Welcome one and all to an exciting new year at Fore Garden Preschool.

We are happy to welcome those of you who are returning from last year, as well as all the new faces we'll be seeing around the school. We hope that those of you who have been with us will help to welcome the new arrivals with a warm smile and helpful word.

For those of you with questions or concerns, we would like to remind you that our ears and are hearts are always open. You may speak to your child's homeroom teacher directly or through the communication notebook at any time, or schedule a meeting with me to talk about any matter, no matter how small.

Please take careful note of the following events, which will help each child and their family adjust to the new school year as smoothly as possible.

August 24th New Student Orientation

All the new students are invited to attend the school from 10:00 a.m. with at least one parent or guardian. You will have the chance to meet your child's homeroom teacher, hear a little about the class and also introduce your child. I will also give a presentation on the school with some important reminders and information about joining. We will finish around noon.

August 27th Information Day

All students (new and old) are invited to attend with at least one parent or guardian for two hours in the morning, beginning from 10:00 a.m.

Each class will gather and engage in some basic "getting to know you" activities along with music, art and storytelling. Afterwards, each class will enjoy lunch in their own classroom and then dismiss around 1:00 p.m.

Please note that lunch service is not available on this day so please bring your own lunch.

August 28th First Day of School

All students will begin their first official day of school in their new classroom.

Parents are encouraged to give a lot of love and support to their children, as starting a new school or class is a big step for any child, and every child will react in a different way. Expect the adjustment period to take one to three weeks. Both the homeroom teacher and principal are available to advise you on this process at any time.

海外子女教育の現状について ①

（出典：文部科学省資料）

1. 海外に在留する日本人及びその同伴する学齢期の子供の数

20年間右肩あがりで、平成元年に34万人だった長期滞在者数は70万人をこえています。

これに伴う海外子女数も47,000人から58,000人に増加しています。

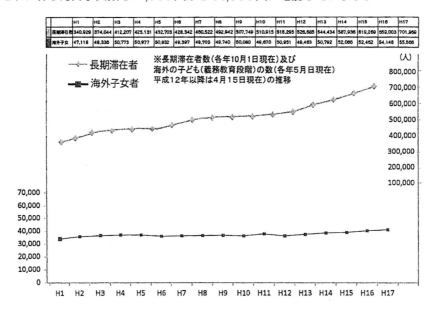

	H1	H2	H3	H4	H5	H6	H7	H8	H9	H10	H11	H12	H13	H14	H15	H16	H17
長期滞在者	340,929	374,044	412,207	425,131	432,703	428,342	460,522	492,942	507,749	510,915	515,295	526,685	544,434	587,936	619,269	659,003	701,969
海外子女	47,118	49,336	50,773	50,977	50,932	49,397	49,703	49,740	50,080	49,670	50,951	49,463	50,792	52,066	52,452	54,148	55,566

※長期滞在者数（各年10月1日現在）及び海外の子ども（義務教育段階）の数（各年5月1日現在）平成12年以降は4月15日現在）の推移

2. 海外のこども（義務教育段階）の数の地域別の滞在状況

アジア圏が38%、アメリカ・カナダ圏が35%とこの2つの地域で70%を超えています。

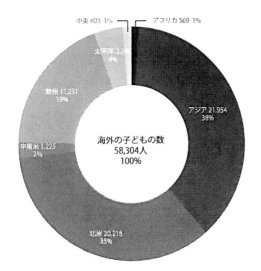

中東 803 1%　　アフリカ 569 1%
太平洋 2,3xx 4%
欧州 11,231 19%
中南米 1,225 2%
北米 20,218 35%
アジア 21,954 38%
海外の子どもの数 58,304人 100%

第2章　園児・保護者との章

Chapter 2　Preschool Children and Parents

入園式の打ち合わせ

 いよいよ入園式が間近に迫ってきました。

今年度の担当のクラスが書かれているリストをすでにお渡ししています。リストには担当するクラスの園児の名前があります。きちんと読んできましたか？

ことに3歳児クラスは半数以上が新入園児です。集団生活が初めての子が大半ですから早く園の日常のリズムに慣れてもらえるように心がけてください。

また、4歳児クラスの多くの子はお互いにすでに親しくなっていますから、そこに入る新しい園児が仲間外れに合わないように気配りを十分にしてください。

はい、どの子も早く馴染んでもらえるように心がけます。

当日は園の門のところで、子どもたちの出迎えをして、新入生の顔と名前を予め一致できるようにします。

それはいいことだわ。最近はママ離れができなくて、握った手を離したがらない子もいますから。これはおそらく、一人っ子が多くなったからでしょうね。入園式で歌う歓迎の歌の練習はできていますか？

はい、みんな大きな声で歌うと張り切っています。

エレクトーンは入園式の前日に会場に持ち込むようにしています。

分かりました。入園式の飾りつけも明日には届きますから、前日にみんなで会場の飾りつけをやりましょう。

雨が降ったときに備えて傘立ての準備は大丈夫ですか？

はい、予備の傘立ても含めて準備をしていますし、傘入れのビニール袋も準備しています。

お子様にも保護者の方にも、幸せで思い出深い入園式になるように、全員がんばってください。

Meeting about the First Day of School and the Entrance Ceremony

We're almost nearing our entrance ceremony.

Previously, I handed out a list with the class you will be in charge of this year. On the list are the names of the students in your class. Have you had a chance to read through them carefully?

More than half of the students in the 3-year-old class will be new students. For most of them, it will be their first time in a group environment, so please make sure that they adjust to the rhythm of daily life in the school early on.

On the other hand, the students in the 4-year-old class already know each other well, so please take care to check that none of the new students are being left out.

Yes, I'll make sure everyone feels at home in the class and finds a place to fit in.

I'm planning on greeting the children at the front gate on the day of the entrance ceremony to get a head start on matching names with faces for the incoming students.

That's a good idea. Nowadays there are children who have difficulties leaving their mothers, or who refuse to let go of their mother's hand. This is probably because many children now come from single-child families. Have you practiced the greeting song that we will sing at the entrance ceremony?

Yes, everyone is eager to sing together in a loud voice.

We plan on bringing the electric piano into the hall the day before the entrance ceremony.

Okay. The decorations for the ceremony will be delivered by tomorrow, so let's decorate the hall the day before the ceremony.

Just in case it rains, is the umbrella stand ready?

Yes, everything is ready, including an extra umbrella stand and the plastic umbrella bags.

Please do your best to make this entrance ceremony a very happy and fulfilling one for the parents and children.

入園式

ただいまより、フォレガーデン園の入園式を行います。

園長先生よりお話があります。

皆さん、フォレガーデン園へようこそ。保護者の皆さん、ご入園おめでとうございます。

この度は、ご入園いただきありがとうございます。

フォレガーデン園の園長の山田です。今日から、お子様がこの園の園児となります。

園では毎日楽しいことをたくさん計画しています。みんなで仲良く、楽しく過ごしましょう！

では、これから各クラスの担任をご紹介します。4歳児クラス『ウサギ組』の担任の鈴木あきこ先生です。鈴木先生、一言お言葉を頂けますか？

こんにちは、皆さん。私が鈴木先生です。今日、皆さんと会えるのをすごく楽しみにしていました。待ち切れずに、門まで皆さんをお迎えに行ってしまいました。

みんなと一緒に遊んだり、思いっきり楽しく学んだりして過ごせるのを楽しみにしています。

保護者の皆様、ご入園おめでとうございます。

当園に勤めて5年目になり、毎年どんどん楽しくなっていきます。保護者の方とご一緒にお子様の成長のお役に立ちたいと思っていますので、よろしくお願い致します。

鈴木先生、ありがとうございました。

では、各クラスに分かれます。クラス名とお名前を読み上げます。自分のお名前を呼ばれたら、大きな声で「はい」とお返事して立って、担任の先生が立っているところに行ってくださいね。

どうぞ、保護者の方もご一緒にクラスの部屋に移動してください。

なお、すでに入園のしおりに記載の通り、来週の土曜日に保護者会を行いますので、ご出席お願いします。保護者会は各クラスに分かれて行います。できるだけご参加ください。

Entrance Ceremony

 We would now like to begin the entrance ceremony at Fore Garden Preschool.

Here are a few opening words from encho-sensei.

 Greetings everyone and welcome to our school. Congratulations to all the parents who have enrolled their children into our preschool.

We are very happy to have them with us.

I am Yamada-encho, the principal at Fore Garden Preschool. From today onward, your children will all be students here.

Let me reassure you that we have planned plenty of fun activities for your children to do every day. Let's all get to know each other and spend a great time together!

 Now, I would like to introduce you to the homeroom teacher for each class. The 4-year-olds, or the rabbit class, will have Suzuki Akiko-sensei as their homeroom teacher. Suzuki-sensei, can you please say a few welcoming remarks to your homeroom class?

 Hello everyone, I am Suzuki-sensei. I've been looking forward to seeing all of you today. I couldn't contain my excitement over meeting you all, and ended up going to the gate to greet you on your way into the school.

I'm very excited about spending time, playing, and learning many fascinating things with you.

Parents, let me congratulate you again on enrolling your children in our preschool.

This will be my fifth year working here at this school and each year I enjoy it more and more. I hope to play an important role in helping you with your child's development and growth.

 Thank you, Suzuki sensei.

Now, we will divide the children into each class. Children, I will read out the class and your name. When you hear your name, please reply "Here" in a loud voice, then stand up and walk to where your homeroom teacher is standing.

Parents, please follow your child to his or her classroom.

In addition, as mentioned in the parents' handbook procedures, we will hold a parent meeting next Saturday. Meetings will be separated according to class. We would like to ask you to attend the meeting if you are not otherwise engaged.

入園式における園長祝辞（要約）

フォレガーデン
園長　山田　ポール

夏の暑い時期が始まり秋の訪れを感じる季節に、新入園児や在園児の皆さんと新しいスタートができとてもうれしく思います。

今年度、当園は全7クラス88人のお友達を迎えるまでに成長いたしました。お子様の人生は毎年新しい挑戦・新たな能力や多くの驚きがあります。各学年で、経験豊富な先生方が、お子様の成長を見守り、次の成長に導いていきますので、安心してお預けください。

一人ひとりのお子様が最大限の能力を発揮するためには、園と家庭でお子様にとってのよい環境を整える必要があります。私共は、保護者の皆様と一緒にお子様が成長に必要な、愛情、サポートと強さを持てるように協力していきたいと思っております。

先生やお子様のクラスメイトと知り合う時間を作っていただきたいと思っております。クラスの皆さんは仲間であり、お互いの距離が近ければ、よりよい関わりができます。

当園では、お子様と保護者の方に楽しんでいただけるように、延長保育・放課後クラブや活発なPTA活動など多くの機会を準備しております。お子様とご家族の経験が豊かなものになるようぜひ積極的に参加・ご活用ください。

私ども園の職員一同は、皆様と最高の年を迎えられるよう頑張ってまいります。ご理解とご協力を心からお祈り申し上げます。

Welcoming Remarks from the Principal at the Entrance Ceremony

As we say hello to the hot days of the summer and begin to look towards the fall and the promise of change that it brings, it is my pleasure to welcome you all the beginning of an exciting new year at Fore Garden Preschool.

Our school has grown to 88 students this year with seven classes full of smiling children. Each year of a young child's life brings new challenges, new abilities, and many surprises. Rest assured that professional teachers with training and experience in each age group are ready to watch over and guide your children through the next year of their little lives.

Each and every child needs a strong environment both in school and at home to reach their full potential. We hope to work together with parents to ensure that each child has the love, support, and strength that he or she needs to grow.

We hope that you will take the time to get to know your child's teacher and also his or her classmates. Each class is a community and the closer we all are, the better a job we can do at communicating.

Also please remember that we have many additional options such as extended child care, after school clubs, and a very active PTA. Please do not hesitate to get involved and enrich the experience of your child and your family through these wonderful opportunities.

We look forward to our best year yet, with help from all our staff, students, and families. We thank you from the bottom of our hearts for your understanding and cooperation.

Paul Yamada, Principal
Fore Garden Preschool

保護者各位

フォレガーデン園は、様々な背景を持つ子どもたちが自分たちのニーズや多様性を認識する場として20年ほど前に創立されました。子どもの成長に目を向け、子どもを第一に考える環境を作ることを考えています。一人ひとりの子どもたちが、自分の道を見つけられる安心で快適な場所を考えています。

お子様の園を選ぶのはとても大変で、たくさんのことを考える必要があります。私共は、保護者の方が納得して園を選択していただけるように、当園の強みや詳細をできる限り明確に伝えるようにしています。これらの情報が皆様のお役に立てればと思っております。

当園のカリキュラムは、最新の研究に基づいており、常に先生が考え発展したものになっています。当園の先生方は、豊富な幼児教育の経験に加え、園からの全面的なサポートのもとで保育に当たっています。

当園には、様々な国籍の児童が在園しており、その数は25か国以上にものぼります。この多様性は登園の強みであり、それぞれのお子様とご家庭が独自の文化を持ち合い、互いに尊重しあえる場所であることを願っています。

また、当園では、お子様の園での様子を知りたい方のために、たくさんの機会を設けています。本を読んだり、イベントでボランティアをしていただいたりと、PTAのメンバーになるた めに、貢献していただく機会はたくさんあります。

よろしくお願いします。

園長　山田　ポール
フォレガーデン

Fore Garden Preschool Brochure, Greetings from the Principal

Dear Parents,

Fore Garden Preschool was established almost twenty years ago with the idea that children from all backgrounds needed a place that would recognize their unique needs and desires. It is our intention to create an environment that puts children first, with a keen eye to their stage of development. We hope to provide a safe and comfortable classroom where each child can find their own way.

We know that selecting a school for your young child is a big decision, with many factors to consider. We strive to communicate as clearly as possible the strengths and details of our school, so that parents can make the most informed choice possible about whether to enroll. We trust that you will find all this information useful.

Fore Garden's curriculum is based on the latest research and is always developing, which is an ongoing process between teachers and administration. Teachers come highly qualified with experience in their assigned age groups, and can expect the full support of the school.

Our student body contains a wide variety of nationalities, with over twenty-five countries represented. Our diversity is our strength and we hope each student and their family bring some of their unique cultural heritage to our school, which will be respected by all.

For those of you who want to be involved in your child's school life, we have a number of opportunities to get involved both inside and outside of the classroom. From visits to read to a book or volunteering at events to becoming a member of our PTA, there are plenty of chances to contribute!

Thank you and I hope to see you soon.

Sincerely,
Paul Yamada, Principal
Fore Garden Preschool

つくってみましょう ②

円を使って色々な飾りを作ってみましょう

園の教室は、元気いっぱいの場所です。園児たちは何にでも興味があって、創造力に富んでいます。この才能を伸ばせる飾りつけにしましょう。いろんな色で彩られ、展示は園児も保護者も見て楽しめる高さにしましょう。園の教室は、ポスターや壁掛け、掲示板、窓用ステッカー等、ちびっ子芸術家のいろいろな作品の展示場にもなります。教室の飾り付けの際に一番大切なのは、園児達の作品を使って飾りつけをすることです。入園式の飾りつけをいくつか紹介しましょう。

【材料】	【Things you need to prepare】
新聞紙	Newspaper
ポスターカラー (6色〜8色)	Poster colors (6-8 colors)
ブラシ、水、バケツ	Brushes, Water, Bucket
タオル、のり	Towels, Glue
園児の写真	Students' photos

円を使って工夫してみましょう・「フォトツリー」を植えよう！

1. 新聞紙で壁を覆います。
2. パレットに色々なポスターカラーを準備します。
3. 壁の背景となる新聞紙にポスターカラーで色を塗ります。
4. 枝を描きます。
5. 新聞紙から色々なサイズに円を切り抜きます。
6. 様々な色でその円に色をつけます。
7. 園児たちの名前と写真を円にラベルづけしていきます。

★ 一度に複数本、木を作って色付けしていきますが、何本かは将来子どもたちの成長の記録を見せられる時のために、とっておきましょう。

Circle Magic! Plant a Photo Tree!

1. Cover the wall with newspapers.
2. Prepare different poster paints on your palette.
3. Paint the background (newspaper) with poster paints.
4. Draw the branches of your tree.
5. Cut or tear off circles from the newspaper in different sizes.
6. Color the newspaper circles in different colors.
7. Label each circle with a students' name or photo.

★ Prepare/paint several trees at a time but leave some of them blank for future use to showcase the child's growth.

Let's Try ②

Let's try and make different decorations using circles

A preschool classroom is a lively and energetic place. Preschool children are naturally curious and creative, therefore, the decor of the classroom should showcase their creativity and challenge their curiosity. It is important that the space should be colorful and that the decorations are placed at a level where both parents and young children are able to see and appreciate them. A preschool classroom can also be a "gallery" of children's artwork through the use of posters, wall hangings, bulletin boards, and window stickers. The main point to remember about decorating your classroom is to use your students' pieces of artworks. Here are few ideas for themed decorations for the entrance ceremony.

Let's try

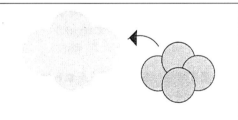

4つの円を重ね合わせて、雲を作ります
Overlap four circles for a cloud

中心の円のまわりに色合いの違う円を並べて、花を作ります
Put circles around a center circle of a different hue for a flower

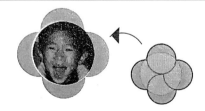

色やサイズの違う円を重ね合わせて、フォトフレームを作ります
Overlap circles in different colors and sizes for a photo frame

円を線状に並べてガーランドを作ります
Join circles in a line for a garland

花壇を作る

来週の月曜日から、毎年恒例のクラス別の花壇作りを行います。

園児はあまり土に触れることがないので、土の感触を知ってもらういい機会になります。

お花のお世話を通じて、責任感と達成感を育てることができます。自分で植えた種や球根が花を咲かせるまでを見る過程で、子どもたちは生命の芽生える様子に関わり、育て方を学びます。

園でお世話をする役目があると、子どもたちは、ママと離れてつらい気持ちも紛れて、園に慣れやすくなります。

今年は新入園児の多いクラスから行っていきますから、ウサギ組さんからはじめてください。

はい、わかりました。ウサギ組は、花壇の10分の1を使って左側にチューリップの球根を植えることにします。色とりどりのチューリップ畑ができるでしょう。

この季節は雨があまり降らなかったので、春一番が、花粉を大量に飛んできます。この花粉は、風の強い日は本当にひどいです。春一番が強く吹くと、乾燥した土が舞って、花粉とくっつき、子どもたちの気管支に障害を起こすこともあります。花粉症や喘息のある子どもたちはマスクの着用を忘れないようにしてください。

わかりました。土いじりの嫌いな子どもは手袋をさせますか？

土いじりの嫌いな子どもは、土に触れたことがない、あるいは土は「汚い」と保護者の方に教えられているケースが多いと思います。未経験のことを体験させるあるいは間違えた先入観を取り除いてあげることも私たち教師にとって大切な仕事ですから、素手で土に触れさせるようにお願いします。

分かりました。では、手袋なしでやらせます。

いったん土いじりをはじめると、子ども達は夢中になって、嫌に感じていたことも全て忘れてやってくれますよ。

そうですね、そう思います。球根ですと種から育てるより早く芽もでます。最初の芽が土から出たのを見た子どもたちの喜んだ顔や、興奮した顔を見るのが楽しみです。

子どもたちがあまり水をやりすぎないように気を付けて見ていてあげてくださいね。のめり込みすぎてしまった子どもはお水をあげすぎて、お花をだめにしてしまうこともありますから。

Making Flower Beds

 Starting from next Monday, each class will be making their own flower bed, which is one of our favorite annual activities.

Preschoolers don't usually touch soil, so making flower beds gives them an opportunity to learn about the texture of soil.

It also helps them gain a sense of responsibility and accomplishment through taking care of flowers. From planting of seeds or bulbs, to watching the flowers grow into full bloom, the children become involved in the process of watching life unfold and learn how to nurture it.

It's easier for children to separate from their moms and become used to preschool once they are given a care-giving role at school.

This year, we'll start from the class with the greatest number of new students, so, rabbit class, please go first.

 Okay, sure. The rabbit class will use one tenth of the flower bed; on the left-hand side we are going to plant tulip bulbs. So, we will have a colorful tulip garden.

 We didn't get much rain this season, and the March winds carry a great amount of pollen in the air. This pollen can be really bad on very windy days. When the March winds are very strong, the dried-up soil combines with the pollen in the air and may cause bronchial problems. Please remember to put masks on children who have hay fever or suffer from asthma.

 Okay. Should the children wear gloves if they don't like touching the soil?

 Children who don't like to play with soil usually have never touched it before, or they have been taught by their parents that it is dirty. It's important for us as teachers to help them experience something they've never done before, or to get rid of such misconceptions. Therefore, please encourage them to touch the soil with their bare hands.

 Alright, we'll have them do the planting without gloves then.

 Once they get their hands dirty, I'm sure they will be so absorbed in the process that they will forget all about any discomfort they may have felt.

 Yes, I think you're alright. Plus using bulbs, rather than seeds, means that the flowers will sprout sooner. It'll be exciting to see the joy and excitement in the children's faces when they see the first green shoots pop out of the ground.

 Please be careful to monitor the children, so that they do not give too much water to the plants. Some children who become "too" involved in taking care of the flowers end up giving them too much water, which can kill them.

遠足の準備

来週の遠足の準備は順調ですか？

はい、すでに遠足に付き添っていただく保護者の方も決まりましたし、順路と目的地の下見も行いました。

当日、天気が良ければよいのですが。

週間天気予報では、晴れのちくもりとのことでした。低気圧は接近していないので、大きく天気が崩れることはなさそうですね。

そうですか。今は遠足には最適な季節ですから、お天気が良ければ、楽しめそうですね。

はい、有栖川山公園には大きな木が、うっそうと茂っているところもあり、茂みの中を自由に走れます。バッタやアオムシ等の昆虫もいますから、子どもたちは本当に楽しんで満足してくれそうですね。

ほんとにそうですよね！モグラやミミズがいたら、子どもたちもびっくりするでしょうね。

色々なお花も咲いていますしね。私まですでにウキウキしてしまいます。

そういえば、あの公園にはハチの巣があるらしくて、何人かハチに刺された子もいると聞いたことがあります。ハチには十分気を付けてください。

そうですね、ハチですか。どこにいるかわかりませんから、ちょっと怖いですね。ハチアレルギーの子もいるかもしれませんからね。

そうですね、万一ハチに刺されることがあったら、すぐに病院に連れて行ってくださいね。アレルギーだった場合、危険な状態になることもありますから。

子どもが、ハチアレルギーがあるかどうか、保護者の方もご存じないと思いますから、特に注意が必要です。

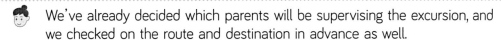

How is the preparation for next week's excursion coming along?

We've already decided which parents will be supervising the excursion, and we checked on the route and destination in advance as well.

I do hope the weather will be nice that day.

The weekly weather forecast says that it'll be clear in the morning and cloudy later on. I'm guessing the weather shouldn't change drastically, because there's no low-pressure system approaching.

I see. This season is perfect for excursions, so if the weather is good, it should be an exciting day out.

Yes, Arisugawayama Park is full of tall trees, and the children can freely run through the bushes. There are even insects like grasshoppers and caterpillars, so I'm sure the children will have a great time and feel very satisfied.

That's very true! They'll certainly be surprised to see moles and earthworms.

There are various flowers blooming as well. I'm even starting to get excited myself!

By the way, I heard that there are beehives in the park, and a few children have gotten stung by bees, so please be extra careful.

Oh, bees. Yes, that's a bit frightening, because you don't know where they are. Also, some of the children may be allergic to them.

If, by any chance, a child gets stung by a bee, make sure to quickly take him or her to the nearest hospital. If the child is allergic to bees, the situation could be dangerous.

Also, it is difficult for parents to know whether or not their child is allergic to bees, so we need to be particularly careful.

つくってみましょう ③

はじめてのガーデニング

植物の成長と観察を通して子どもたちの「これなあに?」を育てよう!
~野外学習~

園でのガーデニング(お花や植物を育てること)は、園児たちにとって観察、発見、体験また植物を大事に育てることの大切さを学ぶとても良い機会です。

園庭は園児たちが幅広く実体験できる場で、積極的に学ぶ姿勢を育みます。花壇の周りに静かに座って花壇を観察することでハチやチョウチョウや小鳥のような生き物に夢中になるでしょう。次第に自分たちと昆虫と花壇の自然な関係を理解するようになるでしょう。

Let's raise children's' inquire through growth and observing the plants!
– Outdoor Learning –

School gardening engages students by providing a dynamic environment to observe, discover, experiment, nurture, and learn.

School gardens are living laboratories where interdisciplinary lessons are drawn from real life experiences, encouraging students to become active participants in the learning process. By sitting quietly and observing the garden, students will soon become fascinated by all the living creature there are, like bees, butterflies, and birds. Gradually the children will begin to see the mutually beneficial relationship between humans, insects, and the garden.

Let's Try ③

My First Gardening Experience

花のつくり Flower Structure

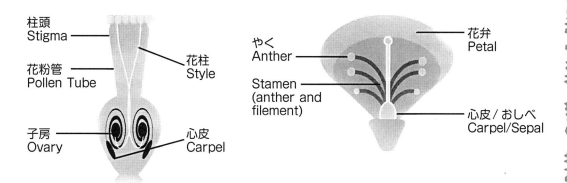

柱頭
Stigma

花柱
Style

花粉管
Pollen Tube

子房
Ovary

心皮
Carpel

やく
Anther

花弁
Petal

Stamen
(anther and
filement)

心皮 / おしべ
Carpel/Sepal

植物の生長 Growth of a Plant

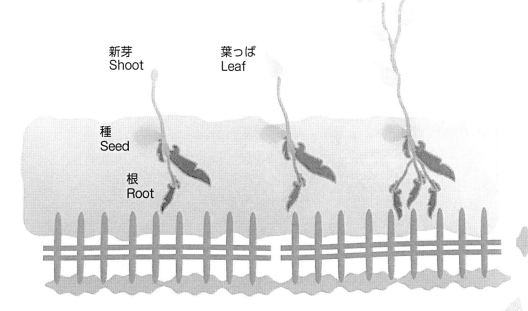

新芽
Shoot

葉っぱ
Leaf

種
Seed

根
Root

保護者面談

では、次に荒木さん、どうぞお入りください。

初めまして、荒木たえこの母でございます。よろしくお願い致します。

初めまして、担任の鈴木です。そろそろ予定日が近いようですね。動かれても大丈夫なのですか?

ありがとうございます。大丈夫です。今月が臨月なので、もう少しで出産です。

そうですか、楽しみですね!くれぐれもお気をつけて、休息も十分にとってお過ごしください。

ありがとうございます。私がこんな状態なので、毎日おばあちゃんに送り迎えを頼んでいるので、なかなか先生とお会いできなくて。

たえこは園ではどんな様子でしょうか?

はい、たえこちゃんはすごく元気ですよ。でも、時々難しい場面もあります。

もしかしたら、ママとの時間が、減ってきて寂しいのかもしれませんね。

やはり、そうですか。普段は、ほんとに優しくて明るい子なんですけどね。

はい、そう思います。性格もとっても良いですし。環境が変わったので、うまく自分を表現できないだけだと思います。

子どもたちは、ママが妊娠していると、本人が知らず知らずのうちに、神経質になって、不安感を感じやすくなります。

そうですね。しばらくの間、気にかけていた方がいいですね。ところで、できるだけ早く通園バスを利用させたいのですが。赤ちゃんが生まれた後は、私がたえこの送り迎えができませんし、おばあちゃんに頼もうかとも思ったのですが、彼女の歳を考えると毎日お願いするのも難しいので。

そうですね。大丈夫だと思います。通園バスでしたら、安心できますし、たえこちゃんもきっと楽しく通園できますよ。

今日、これが終わったら事務室に立ち寄って、通園バスの申込に関する詳しい手続きを聞いていただけますか?

Parent-Teacher Conference

Araki-san, can you come in now?

Hello. How are you doing? I am Taeko's mother. Nice to meet you.

Hello. I am Suzuki-sensei, the homeroom teacher. It's nice to meet you too. Oh, I can see that you are quite far along in your pregnancy. Are you comfortable moving around?

Thank you. Yes, I'm fine. I'm in my third trimester, so I'm almost due.

That must exciting! Please do take care of yourself and try to get a good amount of rest.

Thank you. I've been asking Taeko's grandmother to drop her off and pick her up from school because I'm almost due, so I never get a chance to see you.

How is Taeko doing in school?

Taeko-chan sure has a lot of energy. But at times, she could be challenging.

She's probably feeling sad because she gets less and less time with you.

Hmm, I thought so. She's usually a very kind and happy girl.

Yes, I can see that, and I think she has a very nice personality. I think she may be finding it difficult to express herself well because of the changes in her environment.

Children are also very sensitive when their mothers are pregnant, and, even though they may not know why, they often feel insecure.

Yes. It's probably best if I just keep an eye on her for the time being. By the way, I'd like Taeko to start using the school bus as soon as possible. I won't be able to drop her off and pick her up at school after the baby is born. I thought about asking my mother, Taeko's grandmother, but doing that every day is pretty demanding, especially at her age.

I see. I think it will be okay. As long as it's the school bus, you're in good hands, and I'm sure Taeko-chan would enjoy the commute.

After we're done here, could you stop by the office to ask for the details about signing her up for the bus?

保護者からの指摘

小野さん、どうぞお入りください。

こんにちは、よろしくお願いします。

先生とは毎日お会いしていますので、ひろしについて特にお話しすることがないのですが。

こんにちは。そうですね。小野さんは毎日ひろしくんの送り迎えをされているので、ひろし君の日々の出来事をお伝えする機会があるので、特に私からもひろし君についてお話しすることはないですね。お母様から何か他にご心配なことなどありますか？

あ、ありました。数日前に、緊急連絡網リストをいただきましたが、あの連絡網の順番はどのように決められたのですか？

クラスの名簿順です。何か不都合がありましたか？

モハメッド君のママからの連絡を受けることになっているひろしのお友達のママが、英語をお話しにならないのです。彼女は連絡をもらってもモハメッド君のママが、何をおっしゃっているのか理解できないかもしれないと心配していました。

モハメッド君のママも日本語が苦手で、彼女も同じ心配をしているようです。緊急連絡網は非常事態の時の大事な連絡網じゃないです。何かあって連絡がきちんと伝わらなかった時に何か手遅れになったりしてはいけません。言葉の問題がないかどうか、お仕事でご自宅を留守にされることが多い等によって、作成したほうがいいかと思います。

その通りですね。規則通りに作ってしまいました。

もう一度、皆さんに語学力や在宅状況等のアンケートをして、連絡網を作りなおしたいと思います。

お手数をおかけしたくはなかったのですが、万一のときのためにお話しておきたかったのです。

いえ、ご指摘ありがとうございました。貴重で有益なご意見です。

Suggestions from Parents

Ono-san, please come in now.

Good afternoon.

There isn't anything in particular that I'd like to discuss about Hiroshi because I see you every day.

Hello. Yes, that's true. I get the chance to talk to you about how Hirohi-kun is doing in school when you drop him off and pick him up, so there's nothing in particular that I need to bring up, either. Do you have anything else that you're concerned about?

Actually, yes. I received the phone tree list a few days ago, and I was wondering how you decided the order of the names on the list.

It's based on the list of students in the class. Did you find something wrong with it?

Hiroshi's friend's mom is listed to receive calls from Muhammad's mom, but she doesn't speak English well. She's worried that she won't be able to understand what Muhammad's mom is saying.

Apparently, Muhammad's mom, who'll be the one contacting her, is also worried because of her Japanese. This phone tree is very important when there's an emergency. If something goes wrong, and the messages are not properly transmitted, it'll be too late. I think the phone tree should be made according to whether or not there are any language barriers, or if a parent is away from home a lot due to work.

You're right. Perhaps, I was being a bit adamant about following the rules.

I'll redo the phone tree again after I conduct a survey with the parents and collect information on everyone's language abilities and hours when they are at home.

I didn't want to be troublesome, but I thought I should let you know my concerns to avoid any problems that could arise in the event of an actual emergency.

No, thank you for bringing this to my attention. It's valuable advice and very beneficial.

スクールバス利用申込書 （要約）

フォレガーデン園 バスサービス

フォレガーデン園では、午前と午後にバスサービスを提供しています。当園のスクールバスは、オーダーメイドで作られていて、子ども用に特別に作られたシートベルトと2つの非常口があります。座席にはひとつずつシートベルトが設置されています。バスの乗務員も送迎時や緊急の際に対応できるように常にいます。スクールバスの利用費は下記の通りです。バスを利用の方は、下の申込書に記入し、提出してください。

バス料金

学期毎	週1回	週2回	週3回	週4回	週5回
片道	17,280 円	34,560 円	51,840 円	69,120 円	86,400 円
往復	28,080 円	56,160 円	84,240 円	112,320 円	140,400 円

スクールバスご利用の際は、バス料金は授業料に含まれます。バス料金は、ご利用の前までにお支払いください。

- - - - - - - - - - - - - - - - - - - 切り取り線 -

お子様のお名前 : _____ クラス : _____

自宅の住所 :_____

バス利用の曜日と時間を記入してください。

	月	火	水	木	金
午前					
午後					

保護者のサイン: _____

日付: _____

School Bus Application

Fore Garden Bus Service

Fore Garden Preschool offers bus service both in the mornings and afternoons. Our school bus is custom-made, and it has two emergency exits as well as seatbelts that are specially designed for children. Every child who rides on the bus has his/her own seatbelt. A bus attendant is always present on the bus to help the children during pick-up and drop-off times as well as in cases of emergency. Please review the fee information below. You may then fill out and submit the application form at the bottom to apply for bus service.

Bus Fees

By Term	1 / Week	2 / Week	3 / Week	4 / Week	5 / Week
One-Way	17,280 yen	34,560 yen	51,840 yen	69,120 yen	86,400 yen
Two-Ways	28,080 yen	56,160 yen	84,240 yen	112,320 yen	140,400 yen

If your child will ride the school bus, the service fee will be included in your child's tuition for the term. Bus fees must be paid before the start of a term.

- - - - - - - - - - - - - - - - - -   please cut here   - - - - - - - - - - - - - - - - - -

Child's Full Name :_____   Child's Class: _____

Home Address : _____

Please indicate which day(s) and time(s) you would like your child to ride the school bus:

	Monday	Tuesday	Wednesday	Thursday	Friday
Morning					
Afternoon					

Parent's Signature:_____

Date:_____

フォレガーデン園 ウィークリーメール（要約）

8月31日（金）

保護者各位

とても良い1年の始まりを迎えることができました。中にはまだ慣れないお子様もいますが、先生と保護者の方の協力のもと、お子様たちも少しずつ園の生活に慣れてきました。

次の点をご確認ください。

守秘義務

入園書類に含まれている青い"個人情報"用紙にご記入の上、できるだけ早くご提出をお願いいたします。用紙に記入された情報に関しましては、私たちのデータベースに加えさせていただき、先生方が緊急の際に確認するものとして大変重要なものになります。

準備するもの

保護者用ハンドブックの"準備するもの"をよく確認していただき、忘れ物がないよう登園してください。すべての持ち物に名前の記入をお願いいたします。

登園・降園時間

登園・降園の時間帯は、みなさんが一斉に来園されるため混雑が予想されます。お車をご利用の際は、"フォレガーデン"と書かれた駐車スペースのみをご利用いただき、送迎終了後は次の方が駐車できるよう速やかな移動をお願いいたします。また、お子様を直接担任の先生に引き渡すようにしてください。登園・降園の際は、お子様から目を離さないようお願いいたします。

Fore Garden Weekly Message from the Principal

Friday, August 31

Dear Parents,

The first week of our new school year has been successfully completed. Some of the children are still getting adjusted, but are happy to see that teachers and parents are working together to support their adjustment period. We are sure it won't be long before every child is coming to school with a big smile!

Please take note of the following reminders:

Confidential Forms

Please be sure to turn in the blue "Confidential Form" that was included in your welcome packet as soon as possible. This information is important to the school and is used to keep staff informed of the details of your child's life and is also used in the unlikely case of an emergency.

Things to Prepare

Please carefully review the "things to prepare" section of the Parent Handbook and make sure your child comes to school with everything he or she needs to have a successful school day. Please be sure that all items are clearly labeled with your child's full name.

Drop-off and Pick-up Times

Drop-off and Pick-up times can become quite congested, with everybody coming to the school at once. If you come by car, please use the parking spaces labeled "Fore Garden Preschool" only, and remember to drop off or pick up your child and leave immediately, to make space for the next family. Also please remember to hand off your child directly to his or her homeroom teacher. No child should be unsupervised at any time during drop off or pick up.

PTA のボランティア（要約）

PTA は 1 歳児・2 歳児・5 歳児のボランティアをしていただける方を募集しています。ご興味がある方は、玄関そばの申込書に名前を記入いただき、PTA 活動のお手伝いをお願いいたします。

ご理解いただきありがとうございます。質問がある方は、ご気軽にお聞きください。

フォレガーデン管理部

フォレガーデン週刊ニュースレター

今後のイベント

PTA チャリティー焼き菓子セール・コーヒー

次週 9 月 10 日（月）に、当園の PTA は、登園後に多目的広場において特別なイベントを開催いたします。当日は、焼き菓子とコーヒーを販売し、売り上げは恵まれない子どもたちのための特別な慈善団体の利益になります。また、このイベントを通して、ほかのご家族との交流を深めていただける機会にもなります。ぜひ、ご参加ください。

当日は、駐車場をご利用いただけません。

保護者向けワークショップーお子様と読書をすることの大切さ

9 月 12 日（水）の登園後に、当園の園長である山田けいこ先生が保護者の方向けに第一回目となる子育てについてのワークショップを行います。今回のテーマは、読み書きの能力についてです。もちろん、当園ではお子様にたくさんの本を読んでいますが、ご家庭で本を読むことを習慣づけることの重要性についてお話しさせていただきます。

本の選び方・お子様と一緒に読む方法・読み書き能力を伸ばす方法もご紹介いたします。また、当園の図書館についてもお話しさせていただきます。

できるだけ多くの方にご参加していただきたいと思います。

PTA Volunteers

The PTA is actively seeking volunteers in Years 1, 2, and 5. If you are available and interested in getting involved, please use the sign-up sheet by the main entrance to write your name and help out with the many projects and events the PTA has ongoing.

Thank you for your understanding, and please let us know if you have any questions.

Fore Garden Preschool Administration

Fore Garden Preschool Weekly Newsletter

Upcoming Events

PTA Charity Bake Sale and Coffee Morning

Next Monday, September 10th, our PTA will host a special event in the multipurpose room after drop-off. Baked good and coffee will be sold, with all profits going to benefit a special charity for underprivileged children. This is also a great "Getting to Know You" event for parents who would like to meet other families in the school. Come and make friends and enjoy some delicious coffee and treats for a good cause!

Parking is unfortunately not available for this event.

Parent Learning Workshop
"The Importance of Reading with Your Child"

On Wednesday, September 12th after drop-off, our principal Keiko Yamada will give the first in a series of workshops designed to help parents learn more about early childhood care. The theme of this first event will be a focus on reading and literacy. Of course, Fore Garden students already read many books at school, but research regularly shows the importance of reading at home with family members.

Ms. Yamada will introduce the basics of how to select a book and read with your child, how to use reading to ask and answer questions, how to develop literacy and much more. She will also introduce our library system to parents.

We hope as many of you as possible will attend!

フォレガーデン園「パパと一緒にドーナツ」レポート（要約）

10月22日（月）、「パパと一緒にドーナツ」イベントが行われました。お父様方に、登園後20分部屋に来ていただき、子どもたちとおやつの時間を過ごしました。先生方・お子様・お父様方が英語で話したり、子どもたちの日ごろの様子を見てもらったり、とてもよい機会になりました。

多くのお父様方は、日ごろ園の行事に参加する機会がないため、園での様子を知っていただくために行いました。先生と英語で話すお父様方を見ることは、お子様にとってもとてもよい機会になりました。

今回参加されたお子様とお父様は、すでに次回のイベントを楽しみにされていたので、大変光栄に思います。

今回、無糖・有機ドーナツを提供していただいた PTA の皆様本当にありがとうございました。

Fore Garden Preschool "Donuts with Daddy" Report

On Monday, October 22nd, our classes held their "Donuts with Daddy" event. All fathers were invited to the classroom for 20 minutes after drop-off to join their child's class in a special snack time with donuts. Teachers, students, and their fathers had the chance to experience a bit of their daily school life and speak in English in a casual fashion.

This event served several purposes. Many fathers don't have the opportunity to get involved in the school as much as they'd like. Seeing their fathers interact with the teacher in casual English also set a wonderful example for the children to follow.

We know the event was a huge success because both the children and the fathers who joined are already asking when the next event will be!

A very special thank you to the PTA for providing sugar-free, organic donuts that were enjoyed by all!

海外子女教育 ②

海外子女教育の現状について ②

1. 日本人学校と補習授業校

海外在留の日本人の子女のために学校教育法に規定する学校教育に準じる教育が実施できるよう在外教育施設があり、その主なものが日本人学校です。全日制で、国内の小中学校の課程と同等の課程を有する認定を受けた学校です。世界50か国・地域に85校設置されています。また、現事項や国際学校等に通学している日本人の子供に対して土曜日や放課後を利用して日本国内の小中学校の一部の教科について日本語で授業を行う補習授業校は、世界53か国に設置されてています。

地域別の在外日本人学校

アジア	北米	中南米	欧州	大洋州	中東
32	4	14	22	3	7

地域別の日本人補習授業校

アジア	北米	中南米	欧州	大洋州	中東
16	83	9	54	12	6

2. 日本人学校に関する問題点（回答が多い順）

海外に在留する日本人が子女の教育についてあける悩みの項目の上位に、幼児教育施設の不足が挙げられています。（2005年に日本在外企業協会が企業に行ったアンケート）

1. 高校がない
2. 幼稚園が少ない
3. 学校数が少ない
4. 授業料が高い
5. 安全対策が不十分
6. 遠距離通学・親への送迎の負担が重い
7. 教員の指導方法・授業レベル
8. 企業の寄付金負担が重い
9. 学校の少人数化によるレベルの低下

第３章　新人募集の章

Chapter 3　Accepting Applications for New Teachers

新人募集の条件

 本日は、来年度の職員募集について話し合います。

園長よりこの件についてのお話があります。

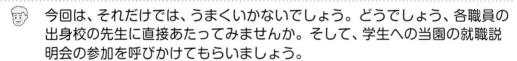 先月、青木先生が寿退社されましたが、来年3月には、石山先生が出産のために育児休暇に入ります。このため、来年は2名の新卒募集を行いたいと思います。

いい人材を確保したいと思いますので、皆さんのご協力をお願いします。

 園長からお話があった通り、来年は2名の新卒者募集を行います。皆さんもご存じの通り、新卒者の就職戦線は非常に厳しいと言われています。しかしながら、幼児教育の分野では来年も人手不足の状況です。

当園としても募集を決めた以上は、卒業予定者の確保に努めたいと思います。どの学校も早い時期に非公式ですが、卒業予定者を明らかにしているようですので、そこに期待したいところです。

前回の募集はどうやって行いましたか？

オンライン広告を出しました。

今回は、それだけでは、うまくいかないでしょう。どうでしょう、各職員の出身校の先生に直接あたってみませんか。そして、学生への当園の就職説明会の参加を呼びかけてもらいましょう。

Requirements for New Applicants

 Today, I'd like to talk about next year's staff recruitment process.

The principal would like to have a word with all of you about this.

 Last month, Aoki-sensei resigned because she's getting married, and next March, Ishiyama-sensei will be taking maternity leave. For these reasons, I'd like to hire two new graduates to become members of our teaching team next year.

I'm looking to recruit and hire high-caliber employees, so I'd appreciate everyone's cooperation.

 As the principal just mentioned, we'll be accepting applications from new graduates for the two openings. As you all know, the job market for new graduates is extremely difficult. But in early childhood education, there's been a shortage of people and next year will remain the same.

Since we've decided that we'll be recruiting for the open positions for next year, we'll try our best to secure two new qualified graduates. It seems like every school releases an unofficial list of their expected graduates early on, so there's something we can rely on.

 How did we recruit newly graduated students last time?

 We place an online advertisement.

 However, that probably won't be enough to meet the requirements this time. Why don't we ask each staff member to approach faculty members from the schools where they graduated? They can ask them to recommend some of their current students to participate in our school's career fair.

フォレガーデン園
職員募集要項（要約）

フォレガーデン園は、有能で熱心な先生を募集しています。ご興味のある方は、
下の詳細と募集要項をご確認ください。ご応募をお待ちしております。

職種　　　：　クラス担任

採用人数　：　2名（3歳児・4歳児クラス）

勤務開始　：　8月20日

勤務時間　：　月曜日から金曜日（8：30 - 16：00）※1時間の休憩も含まれます

勤務地　　：　北東線　麻布駅より徒歩10分

月収　　　：　月給30万円（8月から7月）
　　　　　　　修士号取得者には追加の給与が支給されます。
　　　　　　　放課後のクラス・週末のクラブ活動など、別途 就労の機会もあります。

必要資格　：　四大卒（幼児教育または関連する分野の学位）

その他　　：　音楽に優れている方
　　　　　　　基本的な日本語能力がある方
　　　　　　　パソコンスキル（メール・ワード・基本操作）
　　　　　　　一生懸命で、新しい環境に適応する意欲のある方

応募方法　：　履歴書および能力を証明できるものを郵送またはメールで送付して
　　　　　　　ください。

　　　　　　　書類は英語で記載し、園宛てに送付してください（同時に複数の
　　　　　　　園にメールを送付しないでください）

　　　　　　　書類通過者には、面接のご連絡をいたします。

Fore Garden Preschool
Job Description for Teachers

Fore Garden always strives to maintain a team of strong, qualified and dedicated teachers. Please check the details and requirements below, and do not hesitate to apply if you feel you are the right candidate for this job.

Job Title : Homeroom Teacher

Number of Openings : Two (Year-3 and Year-4 classes)

Starting Date : August 20

Working Time : Monday through Friday, 8:30 a.m. – 4:00 p.m. (1-hour lunch break included)

Access : 10 minute walk from Azabu Station on the Hokutou Line

Compensation : 300,000 yen/month, August – July. Additional pay is available for candidates with a master's degree, and additional opportunities for work are available in the form of after-school classes and weekend club activities.

Requirements : Four-year degree in education, early childhood education or a related field

Additional Skills : Outstanding musical ability, basic Japanese ability, computer skills (email, word processing, basics), a willingness to work hard and adjust to new environments and challenges

Application Process : Please submit your resume and any other documents you feel demonstrate your abilities by email or post.

All documents must be in English and addressed to the school (Please do not submit an email to multiple schools at the same time).

Qualified applicants will be contacted for an interview.

フォレガーデン園
就職説明会のお知らせ（要約）

春季就職説明会

4月8日（土）開催の就職説明会のお知らせです。皆様に当園のことを知っていただく機会を提供するため、就職説明会を催しております。どうぞ、お気軽にご参加ください。

説明日時　：　4月8日（土）10：00～17：00
　　　　　　　※新しいセッションは1時間ごとに開始し、一回の説明会は約45分
　　　　　　　　間です。

場所　　　：　当園　多目的室

申込方法　：　ご希望の時間を1つ選び、当園まで電話またはメールでお送りください。席が埋まってしまうこともありますので、できるだけ早く申込ください。

その他　　：　無料で参加いただけます。ご興味のある方は、事前に申込書を提出してください。

Fore Garden Job Fair and Employment Information Session

Spring Job Fair

We are happy to announce that our Spring Job Fair event will be held on Monday, April 8th. This is an excellent opportunity for those who are interested in working at Fore Garden. Please feel free to come by and learn more about joining our team!

Date & Time : Saturday, April 8th, 10:00 a.m. – 5:00 p.m., a new session will begin each hour and last approximately 45 minutes.

Location : Fore Garden Preschool Multipurpose Room

Registration : Please call or email the school to register for one of the available time slots. Spaces fill up quickly so please register ASAP.

Other Notes : There is no fee to join. If you are interested in joining, please submit the application form separately in advance.

大学や短大への募集を行う1

先生、お久しぶりです。ご無沙汰しております。突然にお時間頂いて申し訳ありません。

お久しぶりね。頑張っているそうですね！

有難うございます。やっと、最近一人前に仕事がこなせているかなって感じられるようになりました。

そう、昔から、あなたは頑張り屋さんだったから立派な先生になると思っていました。まだ、フォレガーデン園に勤めているの？

はい、今もお世話になっています。実は、今日はフォレガーデン園の件で先生に相談にきました。

何かあったの？

いいえ、そうではないのです。うちの園で新卒職員を募集することになりました。

それで、先生に、良い学生を何人か紹介していただけないかと思いまして。

そうですか。あなたの卒業した年もいい学生が多かったけれど、今年も優秀な学生が多いのよ。幼稚園の先生が不足しているからあちこちの園からひっぱりだこなのよ。

自分の出身した学校の評判がいいのはとてもうれしいです！ぜひ、当園にもご紹介して頂けませんか。

わざわざこうして、自分の勤務先のために母校まで足を運んでくるのですから、あなたの園は仕事をするのにとても良い環境なのでしょうね。分かりました、協力しましょう。それではまず、就職課に行き、求人募集企業登録をしてください。そして、本校出身のあなたが勤めていること、私のゼミの出身であることを明記してください。

その上で、あなたの園を卒業予定の学生に紹介しましょう。

Recruiting Students at Universities and Community Colleges 1

Hi, it's been a while. How have you been? I'm sorry to bother you on such short notice.

I haven't seen you for such a long time. I hear you're working really hard!

Thank you. I think I'm starting to get the hang of my job, and I'm finally able to work on my own at a preschool.

Yes, I remember, you've always been a hard worker and I knew you'd be a great teacher. So, do you still work at Fore Garden Preschool?

Yes, I'm still working there. Actually, I wanted to talk to you about something that concerns Fore Garden Preschool today.

Has something happened?

No, not exactly. Our school decided to hire new graduates to begin working from the next school year.

I was wondering if you could introduce a few good students to us.

Hmm, I see. I remember there were many good students in your class and similarly, we have many talented students this year as well. They're in high demand from various preschools because there is such a shortage of qualified preschool teachers.

It's so nice to hear that my alma mater has gained such a good reputation! Can you please introduce your students to our preschool as well?

You came out of your way to talk to me, so I'm sure your school is a great environment to work in. Sure, I'm willing to help. What you need to do first is to go to the employment bureau and register the job openings in our classifieds. Then, write down the job requirements for the positions. Then, specify that you're a graduate from here, that you are currently working at the preschool, and that you attended my seminar classes.

Once that's done, I'll make sure to introduce the preschool to my students who are graduating this year.

大学や短大への募集を行う２

お電話をした、港区麻布町のフォレガーデン園の鈴木です。求人募集の件で相談に参りました。

求人と就職を担当している学生課長です。

お電話でも申し上げましたが、当園で来年度の新卒募集を行うことになりました。ぜひ、貴校の学生の方にご応募いただきたいと思いまして参りました。これが当園の案内です。

来月10日午前10時と正午から園で就職説明会を行いますので、ぜひ学生の方にご参加いただければと思います。

そうですか。ありがとうございます。早速、貴園の募集を掲示板に掲示しましょう。ところで、学生から応募の相談があった場合、貴園のことはどう話しますか？

そうですね、とてもアットホームな園です。大きな園ではありませんが、開園以来多くの卒園生を送りだしてきた伝統のある園です。

職員の勤務年数も平均7年と、他の園に比べても定着率が高く、それは職員同士の風通しがよいことと、伝統があるだけでなくいつも新しいことにチャレンジする若さを兼ね備えている園だからです。

気軽にのぞいてみてください。貴校からも近いですから。

分かりました。希望者がいればお話しておきます。

ところで、応募の締め切りはありますか？応募にあたって特に条件はありますか？

幼稚園教諭の資格か保育士の資格を取得済か取得見込みであることのほかに、当園では積極的に外国人の園児の受け入れを行っていますので、英語に興味がある方がよいと思います。

Recruiting Students at Universities and Community Colleges 2

My name is Akiko Suzuki from Fore Garden Preschool in Azabu-machi, Minato-ku. I called earlier on the phone, and I'm here today to talk about our recruitment for two open positions we are looking to fill.

I am the director of student affairs and I'm responsible for the job posts and recruitment.

I've already mentioned this over the phone, but our preschool is recruiting new graduates for next year. I'd like students at your school to apply for the open positions. Here's a booklet about our school.

We'll be holding a career fair on the 10th of next month, at 10 a.m. and 12 p.m. It would be great if your students could attend.

I see. Thank you. I'll put the job post for your preschool on our bulletin board as soon as possible. By the way, if any of our students ask questions about the position, what would you like me to say about your school?

Well, it's very cozy preschool. It's not big, but we have a long history and have had many graduates come to teach since opening the school.

Our job-retention rate is pretty high too, much higher than other preschools, and, on average, teachers stay for about 7 years. This is probably not because of the positive work environment and long history, but also because we are always full of youthful energy and willing to try new things.

Please feel free to stop by at any time if you would like to have a look. We are very close by.

Sure. If anyone seems interested, I'll be sure to pass on your school's information.

Also, is there a deadline for the application? And are there any specific qualifications necessary?

Other than having a preschool or nursery teaching certification, either already obtained or expected, we'd prefer if the student is interested in English, because we're very proactive about accepting international students.

エントリーシートを確認する

先生方のご協力のお陰様で、来年度の募集に多数の応募がありました。

そうですね。本来でしたら、応募いただいた皆さんに面接に来ていただきたいのですが、そういうわけにもいきませんしね。

みなさんのエントリーシートの内容を検討し、私たちの求める人材に適した応募者に絞っていきましょう。

形式面では、誤字がないか、各項目に定める記載制限文字数を極端に下回らないかを見てください。

内容としては、幼児教育に携わる思いが伝わってくるか、当園で何をしていきたいと思っているのかを慎重に見ていきましょう。

皆さん、一生懸命に記入してくれていることがわかりますね。

子どもたちと関わっていたいという思いが伝わってきますね。エントリーシート4の学生の方は、帰国子女の方で2カ国に住んだことのある方ですね。

本当ですね。カリフォルニアとバグダッドですか。

外国人の子どもとコミュニケーションはかなり期待できるかもしれませんね。しかし、日本語の力が弱いようですね。簡単な漢字が書けていませんね。

残念ですが、日本語がしっかりとできない学生さんは、面接まで進められないですね。日本語でのコミュニケーション能力不足もしくは読み書きの力がないと園児や保護者の方とのやり取りに支障がでますね。幼児期は子どもの教育の一番大切な時期です。きちんとした母国語で接することが不可欠ですからね。

エントリーシート7の学生の方は、シドニー留学経験あるようで、しかも、お父様は外国人の方のようですね。

今回は、海外経験のある学生さんが多数応募してきてくれていますね。

外国語や外国に住むことに興味を持っている若い方が増えてきているのではないのでしょうか。

当園にとってはうれしいことですね。面接に来ていただく学生さんを決めましょう。

Checking the Application Form

 Thanks to all the teachers who cooperated in the recruiting process, we received many applications from graduates interested in our opening for a teaching position next year.

 I agree. Ideally, I would like everyone who applied to come in for an interview, but that's just not possible.

Let's review everyone's application form and try to narrow down the pool of applicants to only those best suited to our needs and our school.

In terms of formality, we should base the review on whether or not there are any typos, or if it's far below the word limit required for each section.

In terms of content, we should see if it comes across that they are willing to engage in developing our child education program, and carefully consider what they are able to provide to our school.

 We can tell everyone worked hard on their application.

 The strongest point to come across is that they all want to be involved with children. Student applicant number 4 is a returnee and has lived overseas in two different countries.

 I see. California and Baghdad, huh?

She'll probably be able to communicate well with foreign children, but her Japanese skills are not so great. She can't write simple kanji.

 Unfortunately, we can't allow students who are not completely proficient in Japanese to move on to the interview stage. Not having strong Japanese communication or literacy skills will affect communication with both the children and their parents. Early childhood is the most important period in a child's education. Being able to properly communicate with them in their native tongue is essential.

Applicant number 7 also studied abroad in Sydney, and her father is a foreign national.

 We have many applicants with international experience who are applying this time.

There is probably an increase in young people who are interested in foreign languages and living overseas.

 That's good news for our school. Okay, let's make a decision about which students we want to ask to come in for the interview.

一次面接１

👦 お名前と学校を教えてください。

👧 はい、南田まどかです。国際子育て大学４年生です。

👦 今日は面接に来てくださってありがとうございます。これから採用面接を行います。まず、プライバシー保護についてのご説明をさせていただきますね。今日お聞きすることや提出いただいている書類は、採用選考のためのみに利用します。

提出いただいている書類は、採用の場合は人事資料として保管します。採用に至らなかった場合は、外部への流失を避けるために、当園でシュレッダーにかけ破棄させていただきます。

ご希望があれば返却もしています。返却のご希望がありますか？

👧 いえ、返却は不要です。

👦 分かりました。次に、採用までのプロセスをご説明します。採用希望される方から提出いただいたエントリーシートの内容を検討して当園が求める人材に当てはまる場合、面接を行います。今日がその面接です。

約1週間後に、面接結果をご連絡します。その後、面接の合格者には、WEB試験を受けていただきます。その結果に基づき、園長の最終面接を受けていただき採用が決定します。

お分かりいただけましたか？また、ここまでのことで質問がありますか？

👧 結果の通知は郵送でしょうか？それとも、電話連絡またはメールでしょうか？

👦 連絡は、エントリーシートに記載していただいているメールアドレスにお送りします。よろしいですか？

👧 はい、結構です。ただ、パソコンを自宅に持たないので、大学のパソコンで確認することになります。なので、メールを送っていただいてもすぐにお返事ができないかもしれません。

何か、すぐにお送りしなければいけないものはありますか？

👦 いえ、それはありません。

Interview 1

 Please tell me your name and the name of the school where you are currently studying.

Yes, my name is Madoka Minamida, and I'm a senior studying at International Childcare University.

Thank you for coming in for the interview today. I'd like to begin our interview now. First, let me explain about our privacy policy. I will be asking you questions today about the documents that you submitted, which will only be used for the application process.

All of the documents that you submitted will be stored here at school for HR purposes if you are accepted for one of the open positions. If you are not accepted, however, to avoid information leakage, we will, in general, shred the documents here at the school.

If you wish, we can return them to you. Do you wish to have them back?

No, I don't need them returned.

Okay, I understand. Next, I would like to explain the process up until recruitment to you. Once we review the content of the submitted application form, we set up an interview with those applicants who fit the criteria for the open positions. The interview being held today is a result of this process.

We will contact you in about a week with the interview results. Then, we will ask those who have passed the interview to take an online exam. Depending on the test results, the final interview will be held with the principal and then it will be determined whether or not you will be offered the job.

Do you understand the process, or have any questions up until this point?

Will the results be sent by post? Or, will I be notified by phone or email?

We would like to contact you via the email address that you wrote down on your application form. Would that be alright?

Yes, that is fine. Except, I don't have a computer at home and will have to check it from a public computer at my university. So, even if you send me an email, I may not be able to respond to you immediately.

Will I need to reply to anything right away?

No, that won't be necessary.

一次面接2

では、面接を始めます。面接は、事務長の私と鈴木先生で行います。既にエントリーシートに記載されてはいますが、当園を希望する理由を述べてください。

幼児教育に携わることは私の中学時代からの夢でした。

幼児の笑顔に毎日触れることができて、それが自分の仕事だと思うとうれしくなります。

貴園は、歴史があり、それは、地域の方々の信頼が厚い証しだと思います。また、先日の就職説明会も職員の方々が、笑顔をたやさず、テキパキと効率よく仕事をされていていました。

温かく、居心地のよい雰囲気の職場で働きたいと思いましたので、貴園を希望しました。

有難うございます。そうですね、当園の先生方は笑顔が素敵で、職員室でも笑いが絶えないことが自慢なのです。

当園では、外国人のお子様も積極的に受け入れていますが、この点についてはいかがですか？

私が貴園に応募したのも、その点にも関心があったからです。

もっと、日本の園に、様々な国の子どもたちが通える環境が必要だと思っています。

幼児期から日本の保育や教育に触れておくと、将来大人になったときに、日本のことを理解していただけることにつながると思います。

このような国際交流に貢献したいと思っています。

その通りですね。南田さん、若いのにしっかりとした自分の意見を持っていますね。あなたのような若い女性がどんどん出てきてくれたら、もっと日本は良い方向に進んでいくと思います。今日はお疲れさまでした。

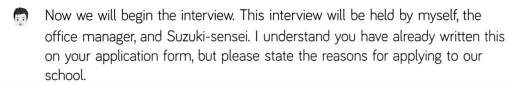

Interview 2

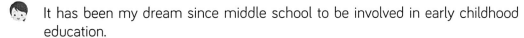

Now we will begin the interview. This interview will be held by myself, the office manager, and Suzuki-sensei. I understand you have already written this on your application form, but please state the reasons for applying to our school.

It has been my dream since middle school to be involved in early childhood education.

Being able to see children smile every day, and knowing that this is my job, makes me very happy.

Your school has a long history, which is evidence that there is strong support from the local community. During the career fair the other day, I noticed your staff were working very efficiently and yet never seemed to lose their smiles.

I applied to your school because I felt that I wanted to work in a warm, welcoming work environment.

Thank you. You're right, our teachers have great smiles and we're proud of the endless laughter in our faculty room.

We happily accept international students to our school. How do you feel about that?

One of the reasons I applied to your school was because I was interested in this factor.

I feel it is necessary to provide an open environment for foreign children in Japanese preschools.

If these children interact with others in a Japanese childcare and education system since childhood, I believe they will have a better understanding of Japanese culture when they become adults.

I would like to contribute to this kind of international exchange.

That's right. Minamida-san, you have strong points of view for such a young person. If there were more young women like you, I think Japan would have a brighter future ahead. Thank you for coming in today.

面接の質問事項 （要約）

1. 当園を志望された理由をお聞かせください。

2. 子どもと関わる上で、最も重要と考えることは何ですか。

3. 子どもとどのように関わりますか。

4. あなたの長所・短所は何ですか。例を挙げてお願いします。

5. あなたは提案を聞き、改善するために努力することができますか。

6. あなたの将来の目標はなんですか。

7. 何か職務に支障がある制限や障害（食べられないもの・できない仕事など）が
   ありますか。

Job Interview Questions

1. Why do you want to work at Fore Garden?

2. What do you value most about working with children?

3. As a teacher, how do you interact with children?

4. What are your strengths and weaknesses? Please give examples.

5. Are you able to listen to suggestions and make an effort to improve?

6. What are your goals for the future?

7. Do you have any restrictions or disabilities (foods you cannot eat, jobs you cannot perform, etc.)?

BC

最終面接

今日は、採用にあたっての園長の最終面接ということでお越しいただきました。園長の山田を紹介します。

園長の山田です。応募有難うございました。

予想を超える応募があって、その中で、最終面接まで残っていただきました。

よかったです。面接した事務長も鈴木先生も、あなたの前向きな姿勢を高く評価していました。学校の成績も良いですしね。国際子育て大学の学科長は私のなかまでもあり友人でもあって、あなたは、学校生活においても率先していろんなことにチャレンジしていたそうですね。

はい、有難うございます。大学生活は楽しく、充実していました。

学科長自身が若いころ海外のプリスクールで働いていた経験をお持ちで、海外と日本の保育方法の違いや日本に取り入れた方が良い点などをイラストや写真を使って説明されていたので、大変役に立つ授業でした。

先生はいつも日本の保育学には多くの優れた点があると話されていました。

保育の現場は、若い人たちが思っている以上に大変な現場です。

私たちは、まだ満足に自分の意思を表現できない園児と、自分の子どもを我々に預ける母親の気持ちの両方を理解しなければいけません。

お世話をしている子どもたちだけではなく、その子たちの保護者のこともです。

両方の不安を軽減するには、毎日の信頼を積み上げていくための努力が必要になります。例えば、「今日の私は不機嫌」、次の日には「熱が出だから仕事に行けない」、そんなことでは務まらない職業なのです。

しかも当園のように外国のお子様を預かっていると、言語の問題以上に、文化の違い、考え方の違いから行き違いが発生することもあります。仕事には、そういう側面があることも理解してください。このようなユニークな当園ですが、当園で働く気持ちはありますか？もし、いいということでしたら、私も職員も歓迎します。

Interview 3

 Today we will be having our final interview with the principal to decide on the status of your application. I would like to introduce you to Encho-sensei.

 Hello. Thank you for applying for one of the positions in our preschool.

The number of applications was beyond my expectation, and from that large group, you have made it to the final interview.

Congratulations. Both the office manager and Suzuki sensei, with whom you had your first interview, have spoken highly of your positive attitude. As well, your grades at school are good. Furthermore, I spoke about you with my colleague and friend, the head of the Childcare Department at International Childcare University, and I discovered that you showed a lot of initiative and took on many challenges by participating in many activities during your student life.

 Yes, thank you. I feel that my student life has been fun and very fulfilling.

The head of my department worked at a preschool abroad when she was younger, so her classes were very informative. She would use illustrations and photographs to talk about the differences in childcare practices between Japan and other countries.

She always described many aspects of Japanese early childhood care that we should feel proud of.

The work environment in childcare is a lot harder than what many younger people imagine.

We need to understand both the feelings of the children who are not able to express their opinions fully, and those of the parents who leave their children with us.

It's not only the children who are in our care, but their caregivers as well.

Additionally, in order to lessen any anxiety on both sides, we need to make steady efforts to build trust on a daily basis. For example, if you feel, "Today, I'm moody", or the following day, "I have a fever and can't come in," then you can't take on a job like this with that kind of attitude.

Moreover, because we accept foreign children at this school, more than a difference in language, there are issues involved with differences in culture and ways of thinking that can lead to misunderstandings. We'd like you to understand this aspect of the job that we face. Considering our unique situation, are you still interested in working at this school? If so, the staff and I will welcome you with open arms.

最終面接

 はい、貴園が他の園と違うことは理解していますし、一生懸命発展に貢献していくつもりです。

また、体調管理には気をつけます。よろしくお願いします。

本日は有難うございました。園長面接は終わります。このあと、採否通知を出しますが、採用の場合、内定通知を送ります。

内定通知後は、何度か事前に当園に来て頂き、入社前研修や入社前手続きを行います。

Interview 3

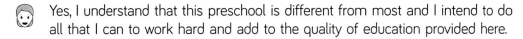 Yes, I understand that this preschool is different from most and I intend to do all that I can to work hard and add to the quality of education provided here.

I'll make sure to look after my health as well. I am excited about the possibility of working here.

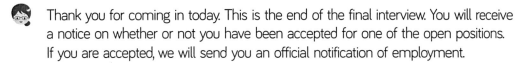 Thank you for coming in today. This is the end of the final interview. You will receive a notice on whether or not you have been accepted for one of the open positions. If you are accepted, we will send you an official notification of employment.

After you receive the notification, you will be required to come to the school a few times for training and to begin the registration process before beginning work.

採用（内定）通知書 （要約）

南田　まどか　殿

フォレガーデン
園長　山田　ポール

当園は貴殿を来年度の4歳児クラスの担任として採用（内定）します。

貴殿の知識・能力・人柄は当園のかけがえのない財産になると信じております。登園の一員になっていただけるように全力でお手伝いさせていただきます。

当園就職の意思の有無を5月31日（金）までにご連絡ください。ご連絡がない場合は、ご辞退していただくこともございます。

ご連絡をお待ちしております。

入社承諾書 （要約）

フォレガーデン
山田　ポール　園長先生

貴園で、働かせていただけることを大変うれしく思っております。採用していただき、ありがとうございます。

貴園の職員として働かせていただけることを楽しみにしております。最善を尽くしたいと思っております。

必要な情報があれば、ご連絡ください。

南田　まどか

Notification of Employment, Sample

Dear Ms. Madoka Minamida,

Based on your resume and successful interview, Fore Garden Preschool is pleased to offer you the position of Homeroom Teacher for the Year 4 class for the upcoming school year.

We believe that your skills, expertise, and personality are well-suited for this position. Please also understand that the school will fully support you in the process of becoming a member of our team.

Please reply to this email to let me know if you will accept this position by Friday, May 31st. Failure to do so will result in us offering another individual the position.

Thank you and I look forward to your reply.

Sincerely,
Paul Yamada, Principal
Fore Garden Preschool

Accepting the Job Offer

Dear Mr. Yamada,

It is my pleasure to accept this wonderful offer to work as a teacher at your school. I would like to thank you for this special opportunity.

I look forward to joining the Fore Garden Preschool team and assure you that I will do my best to fulfill all my duties. Please let me know whatever information or assistance you require to proceed.

Thank you again.

Sincerely,
Madoka Minamida

フォレガーデン園　職務指針（要約）

子どもの健康と安全

職員は子どもの健康と安全に配慮する。その程度にかかわらず、いかなる事件、事故、怪我もすぐに園に報告し、保護者にも速やかに知らせること。

予防措置として、職員は園児の健康記録を把握し、特にアレルギーや慢性的な病気に気をつけること。

規律と行動規範

職員は子どもが安全に過ごせるように日常業務を行うこと。職員は教室や校内における規則を子どもと保護者の両方が明確に理解できるよう説明すること。子どもを適切に見守り、問題が起きた時に対応するのではなく、問題を防ぐような、スケジュール・環境・活動を計画すること。

コミュニケーション

職員間のコミュニケーションを日々行うこと。校長や他の職員からのメールを定期的にチェックすること。疑問が生じた場合は、校長と話し合い明確にすること。

保護者の方と丁寧なコミュニケーションを図ること。守秘義務を守り、保護者と専門的なコミュニケーションを図ること。デリケートな内容は、校長と相談したうえで、保護者に話すこと。

守秘義務

子ども・家族・園の守秘義務を守り、外部に漏らさないようにすること。いかなる場合でも、子どもの写真を個人的理由で、共有・公開してはならないこと。

Staff Responsibility Guidelines

CHILDREN'S HEALTH & SAFETY

Children's health and safety are of primary concern for all teachers. Any incident, accident or injury, regardless of its degree, must be reported to the administration immediately, and parents must be informed on the same day.

For precautionary measures, teachers are responsible for reviewing the health records of students. Teachers must be aware of allergies and chronic illnesses.

DISCIPLINE & BEHAVIOR MANAGEMENT

Teachers are expected to set and maintain consistent boundaries and manage routines that allow children to feel safe. Teachers will clearly outline the rules and expectations concerning classroom and school behavior in ways both children and parents can clearly understand. Teachers will provide adequate supervision and will structure the schedule, environment, and activities in such a way as to prevent problems instead of reacting to them.

COMMUNICATION

Communication between teachers and the administration will occur on a daily basis. Teachers are responsible for checking their emails regularly and reading all memos and attachments from the principal and other members of the administration. It is the teacher's responsibility to clarify any points of confusion directly with the principal when questions arise.

Teachers will address parents in a polite and respectful manner. Teachers will maintain confidentiality and will interact with parents in a professional fashion. Any topics that may be considered sensitive should be discussed with the Principal before speaking with parents.

CONFIDENTIALITY

Teachers may have access to and be entrusted with confidential information concerning students, their families, and the school as a whole. Teachers will not disclose such confidential information to anyone.

Teachers will not in any circumstance share photos of children on their personal devices and social media.

新米先生の指導を行う1

今日から、あなたの指導係をしてくださる鈴木先生です。

鈴木先生、新しく入った先生です。

園内を案内して、必要な職員への紹介や案内をしてあげてください。

はじめまして。

すべてが初めてなので、園のご案内と職員の皆様にご紹介いただけて、本当に有難いです。

また会えてうれしいわ。採用おめでとうございます。

忘れてしまっているかもしれないから念のため、私が、フォレガーデン園であなたのインストラクターを務める鈴木です。あなたと同じ、国際子育て大学の卒業生です。

ここで気持ちよく自信をもって仕事ができるよう、今日から3ヶ月間一緒にがんばりましょうね。更衣室を教えますから、まずは保育着とエプロンに着替えてください。

あら、爪が長いわね。爪は切って、あと髪は後ろで束ねてね。もし気にならないのなら、髪の毛を短く切ることをすすめます。髪の毛が長いと、子どもたちが髪を触ったり、引っ張ったりするから大変なのよ。

お化粧は下地以外はだめよ。

子どもたちとは、様々な状況でどう触れあうか分からないし、汗でお化粧が落ちるとおかしいですからね。

はい、分かりました。化粧室でお化粧落としてきたほうがいいでしょうか?

今日はそのままでいいですよ。今日は子どもたちとの保育実務はありませんから。明日から気をつけてくださいね。これが、当園の毎日の日課と業務の職員用手引きです。毎日やるべきこと、報告すべきこと、そのやり方等は、私から教えるようにはしますが、必ず事前に読んでおいてください。

Training New Employees 1

This is Suzuki-sensei, she will be your mentor from today.

Suzuki-sensei, this is our new staff member.

Please show her around and give her the necessary introductions to the staff and school.

Nice to meet you.

Everything is so new to me, and I really appreciate you showing me the school and introducing me to the staff.

It's nice to see you again, and congratulations on being accepted for the position.

In case you don't remember, my name is Suzuki, and I will be your mentor here at Fore Garden Preschool. Just like you, I am also a graduate of International Childcare University.

Let's work really hard together for the next three months, so that you can feel comfortable and confident to do your work here. I will show you where the changing room is, so please change into your uniform and apron.

Oh, your nails are a little long. Please cut them and tie your hair up. If it isn't too much of a bother, we would prefer it if you cut your hair short. Keeping it long might be troublesome because the children will touch and pull your hair.

Don't apply any make-up other than your base make-up.

We can't expect what kind of situations you will be in with the children, and if it washes off with sweat, well...that'll just look funny.

I understand. Should I go to the washroom to remove my make-up?

No, today is fine. There are no hands-on activities with the children today. Just be careful from tomorrow. Here is our staff handbook on the daily schedule and workflow. I'll make sure to teach you what needs to be done on a daily basis, what needs to be reported, and how it needs to be done, but please make sure to read the handbook in advance.

新米先生の指導を行う2

子どもたちの保育で、私たちがもっとも気をつけなければならないことは何？

子どもたちの安全です。

その通りです。安全がすべてにおいて優先します。子どもたちを保護者からお預かりした時点から保護者のもとに引き渡すまで私たちの1番の責務は子どもたちの安全です。

当然のことながら、園の内外には子どもたちにとって危険がいっぱいです。私たちは、いつも子どもたち全員に目を配り、最悪な状況を予期してそのことが起こらないように予防することです。特に、衛生面に十分気をつけることです。

どのように気を配ればいいのでしょうか。具体的に教えていただいてもよろしいでしょうか。

まずは自分の担当する子どもたちだけでなく、園にいる子どもたち全員の名前を覚えることです。子どもたちそれぞれの性格や行動の特色をつかんでおくことね。

そうすると、どの場面でどの子の動きに注意するべきかがつかめるから目配りの先が分かるようになりますよ。次に大切なことは、何だと思いますか？

子どもたちや保護者からの信頼です。

その通りです。特に保護者からの信頼は大切です。

信頼がないと自分では良いことをしたと思っていても、保護者には否定的にとられることもあります。信頼は一度得ても、わずかな食い違いや勘違いで、すぐに壊れてしまいます。

信頼を得続ける努力は、子どもが卒業するまで続くことをしっかりと心がけてください。

大変な努力が必要なことなのですね。

そうよ。気を抜いてはだめよ。例えば、半年経って保護者と親しくなって、毎日の報告をしなくなったり、報告の内容を省略したり、礼儀をわきまえなくなると、あなたに対する信頼に影響してきます。

それと、会話をするときも礼儀正しくね。敬意をもって丁寧な言葉使いをしてくださいね。それと文書を書くときもわかりやすく、丁寧にね。

Training New Employees 2

What is the number one factor that we need to pay particular attention to in childcare?

Children's safety.

That's right. Safety is our number one priority. From the moment we accept the children in the morning until the moment we return them to their parents, our main responsibility is to ensure their safety.

Not surprisingly, there are many things that can be harmful to children both inside and outside of the school. We need to make sure that we watch all the children carefully all the time, and to expect the worst and prevent it from happening. In particular, we need to pay attention to hygiene.

What should we pay attention to specifically? Can you give me an example?

First of all, learn all the children's names and not just the ones who are in your care. You need to be able to grasp each child's unique character, and understand their actions.

If you do so, you'll become more aware of the children's actions in any situation. You'll know what you should be looking for and how to understand each child's reactions and needs. What is the next important factor?

To gain trust from the children and their parents.

That's right. Gaining trust from the parents is extremely important.

If they don't trust you, even though you believe you are having positive results, they may respond to you in a negative way. Even if you gain their trust at one point, one little discrepancy or misunderstanding can result in losing it.

Keep in mind that your efforts in gaining that trust should be continued on a daily basis until the child leaves the school.

That must be difficult and require great diligence.

Yes. Always stay alert and be careful. Let's say you become close to a parent after half a year, and you stop giving daily reports, leave out some content from the reports, or fail to watch your manners, it will greatly affect their trust towards you.

Also, it **is** important to always speak politely. You should speak respectfully and use modest words. Also, make sure that your writing skills are always clear and polite.

職員勤務規則 （要約）

契約時間・業務内容

勤務時間は、月曜日から金曜日の午前8時30分から午後4時まで。

祝日・園の休みの日を除く。

業務は、準備と指導、親とのコミュニケーション、一日を通しての子どもの監督、スタッフミーティング、その他の園の行事など

出勤

職員は毎日出勤します。もし、何らかの事情で出勤できない場合は、午後9時までに園長に連絡してください。午後9時までに園長と連絡がとれない場合は、お休みする日の午前6時半までに園長に電話またはメールで連絡してください。

当園以外の勤務（外部雇用）

職員は、保護者のもとでの勤務は認められません。通常の勤務時間外の外部雇用は認められていますが、当園での業務に支障がないようにしてください。他のインターナショナルスクールでの同時勤務は、園の方針に反します。

健康診断

職員は、毎年健康診断を受け、職務を健康に遂行できるように努めます。園が職員の年間の健康診断の費用を負担します（年間2万円に税金を加えた費用）。健康診断は、結核・B型肝炎およびC型肝炎の検査を含めます。

教師としての自覚

教師としてふさわしい専門職の資質を備えておく必要があります。
全ての職員は

- 園の職員としての自覚を持ち、園の一員として相応しいふるまいをする。

- 子どもと学校のため、柔軟性・チームワーク力を養う。

- プロ意識をもって、同僚・保護者・関係機関と関わる。

- 教師として相応しい格好をする。きちんとした、清潔で落ち着いた服装を心掛ける。

Job Description and Working Agreement

CONTRACTED HOURS, & DUTIES

Teachers' official working hours are from 8:30 a.m. to 4:00 p.m., Monday to Friday except on national holidays or days designated by the school calendar. The workday entails duties for which the teacher's salary is paid, such as preparation and teaching, parent communication, supervision of children throughout the day, staff meetings, and other school-related activities.

ATTENDANCE

Teachers are expected to be at school every day while school is in session. If teachers will be absent due to unavoidable reasons, he or she must contact the principal by 9:00 p.m. of the day before the absence. In situations when the teacher cannot contact the principal by 9:00 p.m. the day before of the absence, the teacher must contact the principal by 6:30 a.m. on the day of the absence by calling on the phone or by text.

EMPLOYMENT OUTSIDE OF FORE GARDEN PRESCHOOL

Teachers may not accept any employment by a parent of students. External employment beyond regular working hours is permissible but should not interfere with the quality of instruction and duties. Concurrent employment at another international school is against the school's policy.

HEALTH EXAMINATIONS

Teachers will undergo an annual physical examination by a licensed physician certifying that he or she is healthy and capable of performing the duties of the position. The school will pay for a teacher's annual health check-up at a medical facility of the teacher's choice, up to 20,000 yen plus tax. The health check-up must include testing for TB and; Hepatitis B and C.

PROFESSIONALISM

Teachers are responsible for maintaining a proper professional quality.
All teachers will:

- Remember that you are member of the school, and behave appropriately.
- Demonstrate an attitude of flexibility and team work for the good of the children and the school as a whole.
- Exercise professionalism when dealing with colleagues, parents, and the administration.
- Dress comfortably but in appropriate clothing. Dress neatly, cleanly, and modestly.

日本におけるインターナショナルプリスクール
（インターナショナル幼稚園）について

1. インターナショナルプリスクールとは

もともとは、来日した外国人の子供の幼児教育・保育施設（外国人子女向け幼児教育施設）をさしていましたが、今ではそういう定義をはずれ、「英語を使って保育を行う施設」のことを指すことが多くなっています。

従って、インターナショナルプリスクールといっても、一概に同じ質と言えない場合も多く、入園にあたっては十分に検討することが必要です。

外国人子女向けプリスクールは、それ自体が主体というよりも、小・中・高のあるインターナショナルスクールに併設されている場合が多く、卒園後は原則としてそのままインターナショナルスクールに進学したり、母国の学校に進学します。

いずれの場合も、原則として、文部科学省に認可された認可幼稚園で、厚生労働省に認可された認可保育所（園）ではありません。

2. 日本人の就職について

インターナショナルプリスクールは、「英語を使った保育を行う施設」という特色から、英語を母国語とする欧米系の先生方が多いのですが、日本国内にある施設であることや保育の対象となる園児に日本人子女が含まれていることから、日本の保育士・幼稚園教諭有資格者の受け入れも積極的です。ただし、英語力については、かなりの実力が必要です。

（概ね、幼保英検準1級レベル以上）

外国人子女向けプリスクールを含め英語を使った 保育施設を称するの数			
平成20年現在　概算数			
北海道	4	北陸	1
東北	7	関西	58
関東（東京除く）	79	中国	10
東京	101	四国	5
中部	36	九州	13

※当協会後援団体東京インターナショナルプリスクール協会（TAIP）所属校を含む

第4章　園の運営管理の章

Chapter 4　　How to Write a Report

入園式の準備を報告する

明日の入園式の準備が完了したことを報告します。

お疲れ様でした。すべて準備万端ですね？

はい、でももう一度 門から教室までの装飾を確認していただきたいです。

分かりました。門から始めてすべてが正しいかを確認してみましょう。門の飾りつけは良いですね。玄関に保護者用のスリッパは準備しますか？

いいえ、保護者の方には、説明会の際の手紙に、上履き用のスリッパの持参をお願いしてあります。玄関で靴を入れるビニール袋をお渡しして使っていただきます。

それで、靴は式の間、各自でお持ちいただくようにします。

わかりました。そうすると参加されるかもしれない来賓の方の分だけスリッパが用意されていればよいのですね？

はい、来賓者とスリッパをお忘れになった保護者用として、多少余分に準備しておきました。また、トイレ用のスリッパも普段より数を増やしてあります。

そういえば、トイレの場所がお分かりにならない方のために、トイレの案内を出さないといけませんね。あとは式場や教室までの順路と災害時の非常口までの避難経路の案内も必要ですね。

はい、案内表示はすでに準備してあります。今、先生方が壁やドアの拭き掃除を行っておりますので、掃除が終了後、乾くのを待って、貼る予定です。

分かりました。特にお父様や園児の兄弟は、当園に初めて来園される方が大半ですから、混雑して迷子になったり、行きたい場所がわからないと、園の印象も悪くなります。念のために、全ての案内はわかりやすいものにしましょう。

Preparing for the First Day of School (Entrance Ceremony)

 I'd like to let you know that we have finished preparing for tomorrow's entrance ceremony.

 Good job. Is everything set up and ready to go?

 Yes, but I'd like to ask if you can check everything from the decorations on the gate to the classrooms one more time.

 Sure. Let's begin with the gate and check that everything is in order. The decorations on the gate look fine. Are we going to put slippers at the entrance for the parents?

 No, I've already asked the parents in the orientation letter to bring their own slippers. We'll provide plastic bags at the entrance for them to use.

Then, they can keep their shoes with them throughout the ceremony.

 I see. So, we only have to prepare slippers for any guests who might be coming?

 That's right. I've prepared a few extra pairs of slippers for guests, and for any parents who may have forgotten to bring their own. I prepared more slippers for the bathroom than usual as well.

 By the way, there still needs to be work done on the toilet signs, just in case people don't know where the toilets are. We also need to post directions on how to get to the ceremony hall, the classrooms, and for the evacuation route in case of an emergency.

 Yes, all the signs have been prepared. The teachers are wiping the walls and doors at the moment, so once they are done cleaning, and the surfaces have dried, we'll put all the signs up.

 Okay. Most of the fathers and the siblings of the students will be coming to the school for the first time, so if it becomes too crowded and people get lost, or can't find their way, it will leave a bad impression. To be safe, let's make sure everything is clearly marked.

業務日報の準備をする

園児の降園後に記入する日報のつけ方を教えてください。

日報は、職員ごとに準備してあります。タイトルは12ポジの大きさで明朝体かゴシック体を使って背表紙と表表紙に貼ってください。背表紙は縦書き、表表紙は横書きです。間違えないようにしてね。毎日記録する日報の書式は、パソコンのデスクトップの職員共有フォルダーの中にあります。職員フォルダーを開けると6番目か7番目に書式があります。明記されているので、簡単に見つけられます。同じフォルダーに交通費精算書や有給休暇申請書が入っています。

このファイルですか？

印刷ボタンを押せば自動的に印刷されますか？

はい、自動的に印刷されますけど、必ず印刷プレビューで、適した用紙の大きさかどうか、モノクロ印刷になっているか確認してくださいね。カラーで印刷したり、サイズの違う用紙で印刷してしまうと紙が無駄になりますから、気をつけて設定してください。そして、印刷した日報用紙に記入して提出してください。パソコンをうまく使いこなせない先生は手書きで書いているし、操作に慣れている先生は画面上で打ち込んで印刷しています。

園長先生宛のメールに添付でもいいですか？

そうしたいところだけど、それをやってしまうと、園長の受信トレーがいっぱいになってしまって、確認しなければならないメールが増えてしまいます。なので、園長は、指導主事に日報を提出して欲しいと言っています。これらをバインダーに保管して、職員が誰でも閲覧できるようにしています。

Preparing for the Daily Report

 Please teach me how to write the daily report after the children leave school.

 A daily report book is prepared by each staff member to use for their personal notes. Use 12-point Mincho or Gothic for the title and stick it onto the spine and front cover of the book. Write vertically on the spine and horizontally on the front cover. Be careful not to make a mistake. The template you will use to record your daily reports can be found in the shared folder for staff members on the desk top of the computer. Open the staff folder, and the template is in either the sixth or seventh file. It is clearly marked and easy to find. In that same report folder, you'll also find a settlement note for transportation fees and an application form for paid holidays.

 Do you mean this file?

Will it automatically print if I push the "print" button?

 Yes, it will automatically print, but always make sure to check the print preview and see if it's the correct size paper, and that it's a black and white printout. You will waste paper if you make a mistake, print it in color, or set it to a different-sized paper, so please check the printing sizes carefully. After you print the report onto the specified white paper for daily reports, submit it. Some teachers find it difficult to use computers, so they just write their reports by hand, whereas others who are comfortable operating computers, type theirs.

 Can these forms be sent as attachments in an email to the principal?

 That would be very convenient, however, that might overload the principal's inbox every day, leaving her with too many messages to get through. Therefore, she prefers that we submit the reports to the supervisor and keep them in a binder so that any member of staff can view them.

フォレガーデン 教育理念（要約）

フォレガーデン園は、全ての活動において何よりもまず子どもたちを中心に置いています。子ども一人ひとりには、個々の個性があり、身体的・精神的・感情的に尊重されなければなりません。当園は、子ども一人ひとりの理解に努め、お子様・ご家族のニーズを尊重した保育を行っています。

当園の教育カリキュラムは、研究・経験・知識・愛情に基づいています。子ども一人ひとりの年齢・発達を十分に理解した上で、授業計画・教材・活動を考えています。年齢が上がるにつれて、子どもが幅広い分野を学べるように組み込まれており、年間を通して保護者の方にも随時ご説明していきます。

子どもは様々なスキルを教師から学ぶだけでなく、自らの体験を通して学び、学んだことを基に自由に行動することも大切だと、私共は考えております。様々な遊具や環境に触れて自由に遊ぶことで、子どもの活動は生まれています。子どもが最高の経験ができるように、各年齢・季節・レッスン教材を考え、綿密なカリキュラムを組み立てています。

当園の教職員は経験豊富です。子どものことを第一に考え、常に質の高い保育を提供できるよう努めています。教師としてふさわしい行動・指導を意識し、子どもにとってよいお手本となるように努めています。

当園の施設は、子どものニーズに合わせて作られており、室内・屋外に十分なスペースが確保されています。トイレ・洗面台・そのほかの場所は子ども向けに設計されており、子どもが安心・安全に生活できる環境が整えられています。

Fore Garden Mission Statement

Fore Garden is a school that first and foremost places the children at the center of everything it does. All children are unique must be respected on a physical, mental and emotional level. Fore Garden will always strive to recognize these traits and to offer this respect to students and their families in the warmest way possible.

Our curriculum is based on research, experience, knowledge, and love. An understanding of each age group and child development drives our lesson planning, materials, and school activities. Our approach is holistic and focuses on a wide variety of curricular areas, which are clearly communicated to parents as the school year progresses.

We strongly believe that children need both instruction in various skills and understanding, and also the freedom to use what they have learned in an open, self-directed environment. Structured classroom activities are accompanied by free play time with a variety of stimulating materials and surroundings. These are adjusted according to age level, season and lesson materials to provide the best possible experience at all times.

Fore Garden Preschool staff are qualified and well-trained. We put children first and always strive to provide high-quality childcare. As a teacher, we act as a mentor, and role models for all the children.

Our school facility is designed to suit the needs of children, with ample room to move around indoors and outdoors. Toilets, sinks, and other elements are designed specifically for children and are kept clean throughout the day to ensure a safe environment for all our students.

工作の手ほどき（三原色を教える）

先生は、絵を描くことや工作は得意ですか？

いいえ、あまり得意ではありません。

そうですか、工作が苦手なのは苦労しますね。どこの園でもやっている活動ですが、この園では開園当初から、指先の運動を促すことは知能の発達に役立つのですごく力を入れています。

はい、初めて訪問したとき、この園は至る所に先生方の手作りの案内や園児たちの作品が飾ってあるとは思っていました。

どうしたら、上手になれますか？

まずは、色の配色をマスターすることからですね。市販の絵の具に頼らず、三原色から色の混合割合を変えて色調を練習すると、今、目の前に見えている色が単色でないことが分かるようになります。子どもたちにクレヨンや色鉛筆で色付けするときに、1色ベタ塗りをさせるのは簡単です。しかし、光があたれば、黄色じゃなくて、薄い黄色になることや、緑じゃなく淡い緑になること、光が少ないところでは、濃い緑になっていることを説明してあげると物が立体的に見えてくるし、見方が一辺倒でなくなります。

なるほどー。たしかに、同じ黄色でも、褐色に近い黄色から明るいレモン色まで、たとえその色の呼び名はなくても濃淡はかぎりなくありますね。

そう、私たちが園で使う12色の色をすべてやる必要はないけれど、色ごとに白味がかった色から黒味がかった色までの10段階のカラートーンスケールを作っておくと便利ですよ。

わかりました。ありがとうございます。

A Lesson in Crafts (Teaching the Three Primary Colors)

 Are you good at drawing or making things?

 No, I'm not really good at arts and crafts.

 Hmmm, it'll be difficult if you're not good at teaching crafts. All other schools have such activities, but our school started doing so the year we opened, and we focus on developing fine motor skills because it plays a big role in intellectual development.

 I noticed the first time I visited that there are handmade signs made by the teachers and children throughout the school.

How can I become better at making arts and crafts?

 First, you need to learn about combining colors. If you practice making hues that you want by mixing different proportions of the three primary colors, rather than depending on store-bought paints, you'll start to realize that the color you see in front of you is not a single color. It's common to have children color using only one hue when you provide them with crayons or colored pencils. You should explain to them though that when the light hits the paint, it will be light yellow instead of yellow, pale green instead of green, and, when there is less light, dark green. Teaching art this way, objects start to look more three dimensional and they'll see things differently than from a singular perspective.

 I see. You're right, even if it's the same yellow, it can go from a darker shade of yellow to a bright lemon color, and even though there is no specific name for it, the gradations of a color are unlimited.

 It may be useful for you to make a ten-step color tone scale of the shades from white to black. Although, I don't think you need to do this for all twelve of the colors that we use at school.

 Okay, I understand. Thank you.

トレジャーブックの作り方を教える

ずいぶん先の話になりますが、園児たちの卒業記念のプレゼントを今のうちから考えておきたいのです。どんなものだったら喜んでくれるでしょうか。できれば手作りでプレゼントができればと思っているのですけど。

大切なことを言い出してくれました。そうです、私たちの仕事は毎日の保育の繰り返しではなく、子どもたちの成長と発達を常に手伝うことなのです。

初めての卒園式は毎日の成長の証しであり、節目でもありますからね。だから、園児に、その子の成長と発育をお祝いするものをあげることは、すごく良い案だと思います。

わかりました。写真をアルバムにまとめてプレゼントするのはどうでしょう、そうすれば、園のことを覚えてくれています。

それでもいいけれど、それだけだと普通すぎないでしょうか？それこそ、大切な贈り物のユニークなアイディアを考えつくことは、創造力を発揮するいい機会じゃないですか？

写真と一緒にその時々の思い出となるものを一緒に貼ってあげるのはどうですか？

そうですね、でもまだ工夫が足りないですね。まず、アルバムを作るという発想をやめてみませんか。思い出イコール写真アルバムというのではなく、園児にとって思い出とは何?保護者にとっては何？

意味がよくわからないのですが…

思い出って、その子にとっても保護者の方にとっても、大切な宝なのです。だから、宝の本をプレゼントしてあげるのです。

どのページも開いたら、そのときの情景や会話、楽しかったことが頭の中にどんどん湧き出てくるそんな宝の本をプレゼントしましょう。

園での楽しかった時のことを思い出すための本にすると思ってください。

それはどうしたらいいですか？

例えば、園児の好きなプリンのパッケージを取っておいて、日付とか、なにかプリンについて園児が言った面白かったこととかを書き留めておきます。

食べている写真も一緒なら、なおいいですね。パッケージも含めて、少し手を加えてみるだけですごく鮮明な思い出になるでしょう？

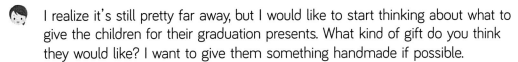
Teaching How to Make a Treasure Book

I realize it's still pretty far away, but I would like to start thinking about what to give the children for their graduation presents. What kind of gift do you think they would like? I want to give them something handmade if possible.

You've raised a very important point. Our job is not simply repeating the same childcare practices every day, but to constantly help the children develop and grow.

Their first graduation ceremony is an important turning point in their development and signals a period of transition in their lives. I think it is a wonderful idea to give them something that celebrates their growth and development.

Okay. What about doing something like putting together a photo album to give to them, so they can remember their time here.

That's a pretty good idea, but don't you think it's a bit plain? Coming up with a unique idea for this important gift is a great chance for you to be creative.

Maybe I could glue some items that represent specific memories from their time with us to go along with the pictures?

Hmm, that is better, but I think it still lacks creativity. First of all, let's move away from the idea of making an album. Don't equate memories with a photo album, but rather think, what do the memories mean for our children and their parents?

I don't quite understand what you mean…

Memories are very special to the children and their parents, very similar to a treasure. That's why you should give them something that looks more like a treasure book.

Why don't you prepare a treasure book that will help them remember specific scenes, conversations that they had in their daily life in the school and with the people that they have come to know.

Think of this as a book that will help them remember all the fun times they've had here.

How would you do that?

For example, keep a child's favorite custard pudding package and write the date on it and maybe something funny or special that the child said about his or her favorite pudding.

This would be even better if you added a photograph of the child eating it. Adding that little extra touch of including the package helps bring back a very clear image of that memory, don't you think?

色彩の基礎を学びましょう

三原色とは何？
What are the Primary Colors?

三原色はどの色を混ぜても作ることのできる3つの色を指します。

The primary colors are three pigment colors that cannot be made by mixing any other colors. In paints, it's red, yellow, and blue.

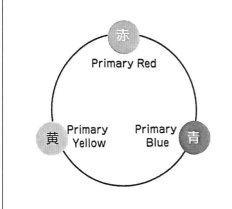

等和色とは何？
What are Secondary Colors?

等和色とは、オレンジ、緑、紫を指します。これらは三原色のうちの2色をそれぞれ色合いを見ながら混ぜ合わせた色です。

The secondary colors are orange, green, and purple. They are created by mixing two of the three primary colors together.

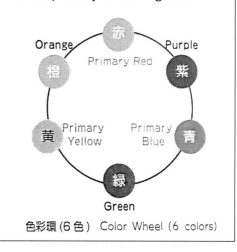

色彩環（6色）　Color Wheel (6 colors)

等和色の作り方
How to Create Secondary Colors

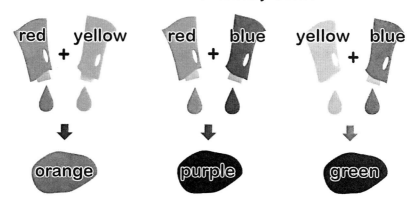

Let's Try ④

Basics of Color Mixing

グラデーションとは何？
What is Gradation?

グラデーションとは、異なる2色の濃淡を段階的に変化させた色（色の段階）を指します。以下のように、赤に加える白の量によって、赤から薄いピンクへ少しづつ変化していきます。

Graduation is the process of mixing two different colors in a series of stages to form the different hues of a color. The example below shows how increasing the amount of white to red, bit-by-bit turning it into a lighter shade (a hue of pink).

色彩環を作ろう
Create a Color Wheel

まず、下の図①を参考にして水彩紙またはケント紙に色彩環のテンプレートを作成しましょう。前ページの色彩の基礎知識を参考にしながら6色の色彩環を完成させてみましょう。

First, prepare the template below on watercolor paper or Kento paper. Then, refer to "How to Create Secondary Colors" to complete the color wheel.

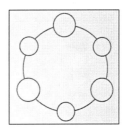

図①　Figure ①

グラデーションの作り方
How to Create Gradation Colors

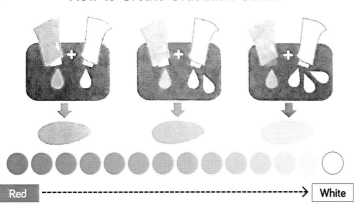

つくってみましょう ⑤

25色のカラーマップを作ってみよう

ステップ 1

図①を水彩紙またはケント紙を拡大して印刷します。グラデーションの作り方を参考にして、25色のカラーマップを作ってみましょう。

Enlarge the template (Fig. ①) on watercolor paper or Kento paper. Refer to how to create gradations and complete a color map with 25 different colors.

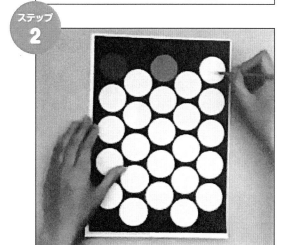

図①
Fig①

ステップ 2

三原色(赤、青、黄)のうち2色を選んで、少しずつ色を混ぜて三つの色を作っていきます。

Choose and mix two of the primary colors (red, blue, yellow) together to create three secondary colors.

ステップ 3

色の量を調整しながら、色を自由に混ぜて塗り進めていきます。

Try to control the quantity of the colors during mixing and coloring process.

Let's Try ⑤

How to Create Gradation Colors

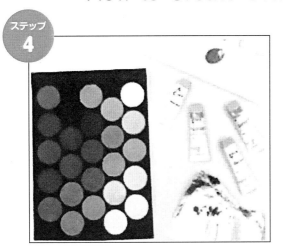

25個の丸がすべて違う色になるように進めていきましょう。
Repeat the steps to create all 25 circles in different colors.

BC

園でのできごとをアートでつづってみましょう
「ジェリーチョコ」の箱からトレジャーブックをつくろう！

●園で用意するもの

お菓子などの空箱/切り抜き、色画用紙か厚紙、クレヨン、水彩絵の具、色鉛筆、折り紙、タオル、筆、バケツ、はさみ、のり

● What to prepare at school

Clean, recycled packages/cut-outs, construction paper or cardboard, crayons, watercolors, colored pencils, origami paper, towels, brushes, a bucket, scissors and glue

●おうちの方にお願いすること

園児と保護者に、コーンフレークの空き箱やロリポップの包み紙、チョコレートの箱のラベルなど、使用済みの箱、雑誌の切り抜きなどを集めておくようお願いしましょう。

● What to prepare from home

Ask the children and parents to collect some clean, recycled cereal boxes, wrapping paper from lollipops, labels from chocolate boxes or any cut-outs from a used magazine is fine too.

この工作の目的を説明します

まず「たべものとわたし」というタイトルを年齢の小さい園児たちには先生が前もって手書きで書いてあげるか印刷してあげてください。年齢の大きい園児たちにはタイトルを自分で書いてもらい、文章も書いてもらいましょう。

Explanation for the Purpose of this Craft

For young children, teachers may prepare the title in handwriting or in printouts. For older children, have them write down the title and some sentences.

ステップ 1 & 2

Pages 1 & 2

●1ページ目〜 2ページ目

「どんな味がした？」「甘かった？」「すっぱかった？」「苦かった？」などの質問を子どもたちにしてみましょう。そのあと、子どもたちが感じた「味」から「色」を選んでもらいましょう。小さな子どもを指導する先生たちは、柔軟で創造性あふれる心を常に持ちましょう。子どもたちの作品をつくる過程には「正解」も「間違い」もありません。

●Pages 1 & 2

Start by asking the children the following questions: What does it taste like? Sweet? Sour? Bitter? Ask the children to choose a color which reflects the taste. Remember that, being an early childhood educator, you should bear a flexible and creative mind, there is no "right or wrong" with the children's artistic process.

ABC

Let's Try ⑥

Making a Visual Journal
Turn a box of "Jelly-Choco" into a Treasure book.

ステップ **3**

Pages 3 & 4

●3ページ目〜 4ページ目
さらに「誰が買ってくれたの？」、「ママ？」
「おじいちゃん？」等の質問を子どもたちにし
てみましょう。お菓子等食べるものを買ってく
れた「人」の絵を簡単にクレヨンで描いてもら
いましょう。感謝の気持ちをページで表現でき
るようにしましょう。

●Pages 3 & 4
Begin with the following questions: Who
bought it for you? Mom? Dad?Grandpa?
Ask the children to draw a simple picture
with crayons about the person who bought
the food items. Let them be able to express
the gratitude in this page.

ステップ **4**

Pages 5 & 6

●5ページ目〜 6ページ目
もう一度自分の空箱を見てみましょう。おもし
ろい形や印象に残る色使いはありませんか？
子どもたちには、折り紙を準備して破いたり
切ったり自由にさせて、空箱を使って自由に遊
ばせてください。

●Page 5 & 6
Look at your packages once more, are
there any funny shapes or colorful images
that catch your eye?
Let the children play around with the
packages, prepare some origami paper for
tearing or cutting, giving them enough
freedom to play around with the packages.

ステップ **5**

「つくってみましょう1」の「2つ折りのパ
ンフレット作り」を参考にして、トレジャー
ブックを作ってみましょう。
Check "Let's Try 1, Create a Two-Fold
Brochure" for details on how to bind the
pages into a mini album.

くまさんのコスチュームを作ってみましょう

【材料】●ヘッドバンドと耳
画用紙(黒か茶色)
10×20㎝のフェルト (こげ茶色)
5×10㎝のフェルト (薄茶色) 伸
縮性のあるゴムバンド

●顔
フェイスペイント (顔料) とブラシ

●胴体
Tシャツ (こげ茶色)
30×45㎝のフェルト (薄茶色)
中綿
タイツ (黒色)
靴下一足 (薄茶色)

【Materials】●Headband & Ears
Construction paper (black or brown)
Felt 10×20cm (dark brown) Felt
5×10cm (light brown) Elastic
rubber bands

●Face
Face paint & brush

●Body
T-shirt (dark brown)
Felt 30×45crn (light brown)
Soft filling
Tights (black)
A pair of socks (light brown)

ステップ 1

ヘッドバンド HEADBAND

伸縮性のある
ゴム
Elastic
rubber band

ヘッドバンドに使う画用紙を黒色と茶色から選びます。画用紙を子どものおでこの幅に合わせて、図のように細長い長方形状に切り、両側に２つの穴をあけ、紙の端と端をゴムでつなぎます。

For the headband, choose brown or black construction paper. Cut a long strip of paper, punch two holes on each side, and use an elastic rubber band to fix the edges together to create the headband.

ステップ 2

耳 EAR

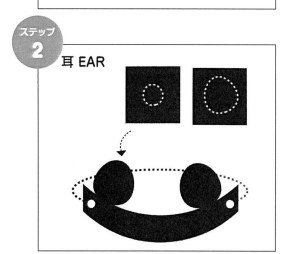

耳の部分は、まず大きなこげ茶色のフェルトを丸く切り抜きます。こげ茶色の円より少し小さめに薄茶色のフェルトを丸く切り抜きます。こげ茶色の円上に薄茶色の円をのり付けします。もう片方も同じようにします。フェルトの耳の部分をヘッドバンドにのりづけします。

For the ears, cut out a pair of circles from the dark brown felt. Cut out a lighter brown shape in a slightly smaller size than the dark brown ear piece you just made. Glue the small circle on top of the big circle and repeat the same step for the other ear. Glue the felt ears to a headband.

Let's Try ⑦

Making a Bear Costume

ステップ 3

ピンク色のフェイスペイント（顔料）で子どもの鼻を塗ります。両頬には、茶色のフェイスペイントで3本の線を描いて「ひげ」を作ります。

Paint the nose with pink face paint. Make whiskers with brown face paint by drawing three lines across each cheek.

ステップ 4

胴体 BODY

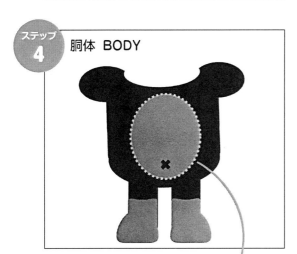

クマさんの胴体部分には、こげ茶色のTシャツの上に大きな楕円形のフェルトを組み合わせます。フェルトがTシャツの前側をほとんど覆っているかを必ず確かめましょう。フェルトにおへそを忘れずに縫い付けましょう。中綿を卵型のお腹の裏側に挟んだ後、「返し縫」もしくは「かがり縫」でTシャツに縫い付けます。

For the body, prepare a big oval piece of felt in light brown on a dark brown T-shirt. Be sure that the oval is large enough to cover most of the front of the T-shirt. Do not forget to stitch a belly button on the felt! Add soft filling to the backside of the oval felt. Sew it on the T-shirt using either a back stitch or over-sewing stitch.

縫い方の基本 Basic Stitches

- 返し縫は手縫いの中でも一番丈夫な縫い方で、ミシン縫いに近いものです。右から左に返し縫いをします。

- BACK STITCH is the strongest hand stitch and is used to imitate stitches made on a sewing machine. Work the backstitch from right to left.

- かがり縫は厚みのある布地がほつれないように、端をきれいに整える縫い方です。布地がほつれないようにスティッチの長さを合わせます。

- OVER-SEWING STITCH or OVERCASING is a way to neaten a raw edge to prevent heavyweight fabrics from fraying. Adjust the stitch lengths so that the fabric does not fray.

B C

救急救命法を学ぶ

園児の救急救命のやり方を学習してきましたか？

はい、2つの授業を大学で取りましたが、救急救命法の実技講習は、インターンと重なって受講できませんでした。

当園では毎年、専門の方に来ていただいて小児救急救命の方法の講習会を行います。もうじきありますが、その前に、念のために私が知っていることを教えますね。

小児、乳児の心肺蘇生法の手順は成人のものと似ていますが、心臓マッサージはやり方が少し異なりますから頭にいれておいてください。小児の場合は、片手もしくは両手の手の平の1/3を使って胸を圧迫します。乳児の場合は、中指と薬指の2本を使って行い、指先は若干足先の方を向けて、胸の中心を圧迫します。

乳児の意識の有無を調べる場合は、足裏をくすぐるのが一番よいです。

1歳未満の乳児には、AED は使えず、1 ～ 8歳までの小児の場合は、小児用パットを使うことが望ましいとされています。

先生、救急救命法をよくご存じなのですね。。

もちろんです。私たちの最も重要な使命は、園児の安全ですからね。

どんな事態にも対処できるように備えておかなければなりません。

救急車が来るまで救命措置をやり続けて大切な命を守ります。

敏速かつ確実に行えるように、何度も練習して、体で覚えておくことが肝心です。

救急救命法は知識として持っていただけでは、とっさのときに役立ちませんから。練習するなら、保育室に練習用のお人形があります。

はい、ぜひ練習させてください。

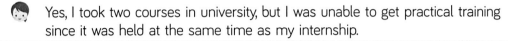

Have you studied the first-aid emergency procedures required for nursery school children?

Yes, I took two courses in university, but I was unable to get practical training since it was held at the same time as my internship.

Our nursery school invites a first-aid professional once a year to provide training sessions for children's emergency first-aid procedures. We will be holding another session soon, but I will teach you what I know for now, to be on the safe side.

Cardio-Pulmonary Resuscitation (CPR) procedures for children and infants are similar to those for adults, but please keep in mind that cardiac massage techniques differ slightly. For children, pump their chest using about one-third of your palm, you can use either one or both hands. For infants, use only two fingers, the third and the fourth fingers, and put pressure at a point in the middle of their chest, with your fingertips pointing slightly towards the feet.

Tickle the bottom of their feet is the best way to see whether a child is conscious or not.

Do not use an AED for infants under the age of one, and ideally, use a children's pad for children between the ages of one to eight.

You certainly know a lot about the first-aid procedures.

Of course. Our most important mission is to ensure the safety of the children at our nursery school.

We have to be prepared to handle any kind of an emergency.

We do our best to protect them by performing CPR and first-aid until the ambulance arrives.

It is important to practice the procedure a number of times to learn the proper techniques and to be able to administer them quickly and effectively

Just having the knowledge alone will do you no good in the event of emergency. We have a training doll in the nursery room if you would like to practice these procedures.

Yes, I think that is a very good idea.

救急救命法

子どもが反応しないなどの緊急事態の時は、次の指示に従ってください。
※2歳~8歳が対象

呼吸

子どもを仰向けにして顔に耳を近づけます。注意して見る・聴く・感じる。子どもが呼吸をしていない場合、救急隊に連絡して、直ちに処置を開始してください。

胸部圧迫

手を開いて子どもの胸部の真ん中に置きます（図①を参照）肘と肩を固定し、胸部を1/3下に押します。1.5秒のペースで30回繰り返します。

図①

人工呼吸

指で鼻をつまんで、子どもの口に口をかぶせます。息を強く吹き込んでください。胸をみて、肺が膨らむことを確認してください。これを2回繰り返します。

AED

AEDが利用可能な場合は、子どもの胸部に取り付けます。子ども用は、青のパッドを使ってください。（大人用は黄色です）片方のパッドが心臓を覆い、もう一方のパッドは左側に取り付けます（図②を参照）。あなたと患者（子ども）の間に水や金属面がないことを確認してください。AEDの電源を入れて、注意深く指示に従ってください。

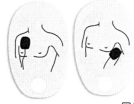

図②

乳児が反応しないなどの緊急事態の時は、次の指示に従ってください。
※生後23か月未満児

呼吸

子どもをやさしく仰向けにして顔に耳を近づけます。注意して見る・聴く・感じる。子どもが呼吸をしていない場合、救急隊に連絡して、直ちに処置を開始してください。

胸部圧迫

2本指を子どもの胸部の真ん中に置きます（図③を参照）慎重に胸部を1/3下に押します。1.5秒のペースで30回繰り返します。

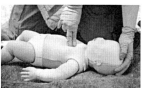

図③

人工呼吸

口を子どもの口と鼻を覆うように置きます。息をやさしく吹き込んでください。胸をみて、肺が膨らむことを確認してください。これを2回繰り返します。

AED

AEDが利用可能な場合は、子どもの胸部に取り付けます。子ども用は、青のパッドを使ってください。（大人用は黄色です）片方のパッドを胸部の中央部に取り付け、もう一方のパッドを背中に取り付けます。（図④を参照）あなたと患者の間に水と金属面がないことを確認してください。AEDの電源を入れて、注意深く指示に従ってください。

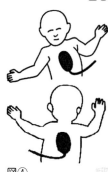

図④

Child CPR, AED Usage

Please follow these instructions if you find a child unresponsive or in a medical emergency. *Note that this care guide defines a "child" as between two and eight years old.*

Breathing

Place the child on his or her back and place your ear near their face. Look, listen and feel carefully. If the child is not breathing, contact emergency services and begin the procedure immediately.

Chest Compressions

Place your open hand on the center of the child's chest (see Figure ①). Lock your elbows and shoulders and push the chest down 1/3. Repeat 30 times at a pace of approximately 1.5 seconds/push.

Figure ①

Rescue Breaths

Use your fingers to pinch close the nose and create a seal around the child's mouth with your own mouth. Blow in strongly. Watch the chest to make sure the lungs inflate. Do this twice.

AED

If an AED device is available, attach it to the child's chest. Please be sure to use the blue-colored pads, which are for children (adult pads are yellow). One pad should go over the heart while the other goes on the left side (see Figure ②). Make sure there is no water or metal surface between you and the patient. Turn on the AED and follow instructions carefully.

Figure ②

Please follow these instructions if you find an infant unresponsive or in a medical emergency. *Note that this care guide defines an "infant" as 23 months old or younger.*

Breathing

Gently place the infant on his or her back on the floor and place your ear near their face. Look, listen, and feel carefully. If the infant is not breathing, contact emergency services and begin the procedure immediately.

Chest Compressions

Use two fingers placed over the center of the infant's chest (see Figure ③). Carefully but firmly push the chest down 1/3. Repeat 30 times at a pace of approximately 1.5 seconds/push.

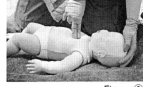

Figure ③

Rescue Breaths

Place your mouth over both the infant's mouth and nose, creating a seal around the lower half of the face. Blow in gently. Watch the chest to make sure the lungs inflate. Do this twice.

AED

If an AED device is available, attach it to the infant's chest. Please be sure to use the blue-colored pads, which are for children (adult pads are yellow). One pad should go over the center of the chest while the other goes on the back (see Figure ④). Make sure there is no water or metal surface between you and the patient. Turn on the AED and follow instructions carefully.

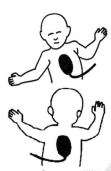

Figure ④

悩みを相談する

今、お時間よろしいですか？　ご相談したいことがあるのですが。

いいですよ。ここで話しづらいなら、会議室で話しましょうか。

はい、ありがとうございます。クラスの子どもたちが私の話をおとなしく聞いてくれないのです。

特に聞いてくれないのはどういうときですか?

特にこういうときという訳ではないです。園児たちが全く言うことを聞いてくれないのです。遊戯の間、席に座るように言っても、お昼の前に手を洗ってくるように言っても、おしゃべりしないで食べるように言っても、私の言うことを聞いてくれないのです！すごく、つらいのです。

それは大変ですね。いつからですか？

私が1人でクラスを担当するようになってからずーっとなんです。

それは困りましたね。保護者の方からは何も言われていないですか？

昨日、ある保護者の方から、『子どもが、園が面白くないと言っていますが、何か変わったことがありましたか』と言われました。

そうですか。保護者の方から言われたとなると、早く解決した方がいいですね。今日のお昼ご飯の時間から様子を見てみてもう少し状況を把握してみましょう。

もしかしたら、一緒に解決法を見出せるかもしれません、いいですか？

よろしくお願いします。

Talking to Someone about their Problems

I was wondering if you have a free moment? There's something I'd like to discuss with you.

Sure. If you'd feel more comfortable talking about it privately, we can go into the meeting room.

Yes, thank you. The problem is that the children in my class don't listen to me obediently.

Can you tell me when, in particular, they don't listen to you?

There isn't one particular time. They don't listen to me, at all. Not when I ask them to sit during dance time. Not when I tell them to wash their hands before lunch. I ask them not to talk while they are eating, but they simply will not listen to me! It is very frustrating.

That sounds like a difficult situation. Can you tell me when this started happening?

Since I asked to be in charge of the class by myself.

Oh, that's a problem. Have the parents spoken to you about this?

Yesterday, one of the parents told me, "My child said that school is not fun, and I am wondering if something has changed?"

I see. If a parent brings it up, something needs to be done quickly. I'll observe your class from lunchtime today to get a better understanding of the situation.

Perhaps together we might be able to figure things out, okay?

Thank you.

新米先生に改善点をアドバイスする

南田先生、ちょっといいですか？

はい、構いません。

昨日、お話したようにクラスの様子を見ていました。たしかに子どもたちは先生の話を聞いていませんね。他のクラスに比べてうるさいし、落ち着きがないですね。

はい、やはりそうですよね。どうしたらいいでしょうか。

どうしたらいいかについて、正解はありませんが、あなたが子どもたちとやり取りしている様子を見て感じたことがあります。

子どもたちがあなたの方を向いていないですね。あなたのことを気にしている様子もなく、あなたが何を感じているかもわかっていないようでした。

どういうことでしょうか？

もしかしたら、子どもたちが何をしたいか考えないで自分が必要と思うことだけや自分が考える子どもたちがやったら楽しいと思うことだけをやっていないですか？その上に、言うことを聞かないからと、必要以上に大きな声で注意していませんか？

まるでヒステリックになったママのようでしたよ。

そうですか？そんなことないです。私は一生懸命にやっています。

わかりますよ。その気負いが空回りして、子どもたちを戸惑わせているのです。

いいですか、あなたは子どもたちのママではないのです。子どもと母親との間には絶対的な信頼関係があるんです。

最初から信頼関係がある母親との関係と、私たちとの関係は違います。私たちは何もないところから信頼関係を築かなければならない。園児たちは、不安に思いながら母親から離れて、園に来て一生懸命うまくやらなきゃと思っているんです。どうやって、お友達と仲良くしよう、どうやって先生に好かれようかと、頑張っています。それなのに、子どもたちに命令をしたり、何度も大きな声で言うことを聞かせようとしたり、急かせたら、子どもたちは心を閉ざしてしまいますよ。その代わりに、子どもたちが頑張って努力していること、お友達と仲良くしようとしているところを見てあげないとね。

もっと、子どものことをまっすぐに見て、ほめて、笑いかけて、寄り添って見守ってあげて。そうしたら、子どもは心をひらいて、あなたを受け入れてくれますよ。

Giving Advice on a Problem

 Minamida-sensei, do you have a moment?

 Sure.

 I observed your class yesterday per our conversation. As you said, the children were not listening to you. Compared to other classes, they are noisy and restless.

 I'm not surprised you would think so. What do you think I should do?

 There's no right answer, but there is one thing I noticed while I was watching you interact with the children.

The children do not face you and it looks to me as though they don't care about you or how you are feeling.

 What do you mean?

 Is it possible that you are not thinking about what the children want and doing only what you feel is necessary or fun to do? On top of that, might you be reprimanding them in a voice louder than is necessary?

You were like a hysterical mother.

 Really? That doesn't sound right. I'm doing my best.

 I can see that, but your enthusiasm is just making you go in circles and is confusing the children.

Listen, you're not the children's mother. The children and their mothers have an unconditional, trusting relationship.

There is a huge difference between a trusting relationship with a mother, and our relationship with them. In our case, we have to build that trust from ground zero. The children are nervous about leaving their mothers and coming to the school, and they are trying their best at doing well. They're making an effort to make friends, and to be liked by their teachers. If you're always giving commands, trying to get their attention by raising your voice, and making them rush about, they will shut you out of their minds. Instead you need to focus on how much effort the children are putting in, in trying to fit in and get along with each other.

Please try to look directly at the children, praise them, smile at them, and watch them closely. Then, the children will open up to you and accept you.

噛む・たたく・蹴る・投げる

攻撃的な行動（噛む・たたく・蹴る・投げるなど）は、乳幼児期の子どもにとっては珍しいことではありません。多くの場合、子どもがまだ自分の感情（欲求不満、怒り、嫉妬、疲れなど）を言葉で表現できないために起こります。このような行動は、前触れやきっかけもなく起こる場合があります。

攻撃的な行動が起こった場合、先生は迅速かつ冷静に対応します。子どもとクラスのお約束をしっかりと確認します。先生はその場の状況を判断し、けがをさせてしまった子どもを離し、怪我をした子どもを安心させて、手当をします。子どもの攻撃的な行動を抑えられるよう様々な援助をしても攻撃的な行動が続く場合は、保護者の方に面接をしていただく場合もあります。

子供が意図的に他の子供を身体的傷害または精神的外傷のいずれかによって傷つけた場合、くわしく調査を行い、問題を解決するようにします。このためには、関係者全員の理解と協力が必要です。次の場合は、退園していただくこともあります。

- 危険な行動が続いて、他の子どもに危険を及ぼすとき

- 園が子供の要求を満たすことができず、専門家の助けが必要と思われるとき

- 保護者が協力的でないとき

くわしく調査・審議を行い、園として最終的な判断をします。

Biting, Hitting, Kicking, Throwing

Incidents of aggression such as biting, hitting, kicking and throwing things are not uncommon in the early childhood setting. In many cases, these incidents occur because the child is not yet able to express his or her feelings (frustration, anger, jealousy, fatigue and so on) in words. Sometimes these incidents occur without warning or provocation.

When acts of aggression occur, the teachers will act promptly and calmly to intercept them. The child will be firmly reminded of the class rules. The teachers will remove the aggressor from the situation and offer comfort and first aid to the injured child. Parents will be notified of the incident. When acts of aggression continue despite all attempts to help the child refrain from them, parents may be called in for consultation.

When a child intentionally hurts another child through either physical injury or emotional trauma, a thorough investigation will occur, and an attempt will be made to resolve the conflict. This requires the cooperation and understanding of all parties concerned. However, parents will be requested to, and must, withdraw their child when:

- A child continuously endangers the safety of other children.

- The school cannot meet the needs of a child and professional help is deemed necessary.

- Parents prove difficult and uncooperative.

After thorough investigation and deliberation with all people concerned, the school retains the right to make a final decision.

子どもの行動　指導方針

規律

子どもの社会的・感情的な学びはとても重要です。当園の教師は、子どもが善悪の判断を身につけ、他の人の要求や感情を理解できるよう援助し、促します。友だちや大人との関わりの中で、対立が生じた場合は、子ども自らが対人関係を学ぶ良い機会になると考えています。

指針

- 子どもたちは、クラスの規則と対応についての明確な指針が示されます
- 一人ひとりの子どもは、個人として尊重されます。個々の出来事は画一的なものではなく個別のものとして対応します。
- 良いことと悪いことは、それぞれの子どもの状況に合わせて決められ、優しさをもってしっかりと子どもに伝え指導します。
- 子どもたちは自分の行動による結果を通して学べるよう援助されます。
- 教師は、子どもの行動を前向きに促し、自制心をもてるよう援助し、問題解決できるよう援助します。
- 身体的・精神的な罰はいかなる状況でも許されません。

特別支援教育を必要とする場合の手順

子どもの世話をする者・環境は、子どもの情緒の安定と知的な成長のために、十分な愛情・安らぎ・安全を提供することが重要です。子どもの社会情緒的・身体的・その他のニーズを満たすよう努めます。子どもの発達において、学習障害や他の問題（課題）が入園後に発覚することもあります。これらの課題は、当園が提供できるもの以上に専門的な指導が必要です。このような場合、当園は、保護者に専門家の助言や診断を仰ぐように勧めます。潜在的な問題を早期に発見することが、子どもにとって最善であると考えているからです。そのような場合の手続きは、以下の通りです。

- 教師は定期的に起こる特異行動を観察し、記録します。
- 園長は記録に目を通します。
- 教師と園長で話し合いを行います。
- 保護者・教師・園長で面談を行い、問題（行動）について話し合います。
- 観察と記録を継続します。
- 専門家による診断をお願いすることもあります。
- 園からの要請があった場合、保護者は30日以内に専門家の診断を受ける必要があります。
- 専門家による診断を求める園の要請に反した場合、退園をお願いすることもあります。
- 専門家の診断結果は、保護者と園長で共有します。
- 保護者・教師・園長は診断結果について話し合います。
- 子どもの個々のニーズを満たすように努めても、改善できない場合は、退園をお願いすることもあります。

Fore Garden Behavior Policy, Special Needs Policy

Discipline Policy

A child's social and emotional learning is critical to academic success. Our teachers are eager to help guide children to develop an internal sense of right and wrong and support their awareness of the needs and feelings of others. When conflicts arise among children's interpersonal relationships, either with peers or adults, we regard them as opportunities for children to learn positive ways of resolving them.

Guidelines

- Children are given clear guidelines about class rules and corresponding consequences.
- Each child will be respected as an individual. Each incident will be treated as an individual situation.
- Reasonable limits will be set for each child. Limits will be stated kindly but firmly.
- Children will be encouraged to learn through the consequences of their behavior.
- Teachers take positive action to direct or re-direct children's behavior, help the children regain self-control, and guide them to solve their own problems by acting as mediators.
- Physical or mental punishment is not tolerated under any circumstances.

Procedures Taken When Special Needs Education is Required

It is important that a child's caregivers and environment provide the love, comfort, and security essential for emotional stability and intellectual growth. We are aware of the socio-emotional, physical, and other needs of the children in our care. Sometimes in a child's development, learning disabilities or other challenges arise after a child is admitted to a preschool. These challenges may be of such a nature that they require more specialized and professional guidance than what Fore Garden Preschool is able to provide. In these cases, we reserve the right to recommend that parents seek professional advice and/or a diagnosis. This is done in the belief that early detection of a potential problem is the best and most loving way to do what is best for the child. The procedure we follow in such cases is:

- Teachers observe and document out-of-the ordinary behavior that occurs on a regular basis.
- The principal reviews documentation.
- Teachers discuss the documentation with the principal.
- Parents, the teacher and the Principal will hold a meeting to discuss the documentation.
- Observation and documentation continue in the classroom.
- Parents may be asked to have their child assessed by a specialist.
- Parents have 30 days to comply with the request for further evaluation.
- The school reserves the right to ask parents to withdraw the child for non-compliance with the school's request to seek a professional assessment.
- The results of professional assessments will be shared by the parents with the principal.
- Parents, teachers and the principal will meet together to discuss the assessment.
- While all efforts will be made to best meet the individual needs of each child, the school may recommend that a child withdraw from the school if it is unable to meet those needs.

BC

文章作成を指導する

南田先生、今年の遠足についての保護者の方向けのお手紙は作りましたか？

はい。一応作りましたが、うまくできなくて。見てもらえませんか。

いいですよ。多くの先生が、保護者への連絡事項を書くのに苦労しています。大学では、就職後に作成するメールの内容や、文章構成を教えてくれませんからね。それに、日常生活でも文章を書くことがないから、入園したてのころは、上手に書けないものですよ。

文章を書くときの敬語の使い方が苦手で。

そのようですね、この文章はひどいですね。内容よりも先に、誤字脱字が多すぎますね。パソコンのワード変換で出てきた文字をそのまま使ったんですね。それに、書き終わってから読み直しましたか？句読点もないし、脱字もしているから言葉になっていないところもありますね。

あなたの名前で出す手紙や文章でも、園のクラス担任として出すものは、園を代表して出しています。保護者の方は、その内容を見て園全体の評価をするのです。ひどい文章、ましてや誤字脱字がある手紙や書類を受け取ると、こんなレベルの園にわが子を預けていて大丈夫かと不安になるし、あなた1人のために、園の評価も下がって迷惑をかけることになるのですよ。

すみません。

それから、話し言葉で文章を書いてはだめですよ。もちろん、園児の会話の内容を直接話法で書くならそれでもいいです。しかし、間接話法で書くなら、文語調に置き換えて、接続詞を付けないと。それから内容が変わるところは、段落を変えないといけないですね。

それに、余分な修飾語が多すぎます。保護者の方はお忙しいから、読む時間が短くて済むように、言いたいことや、お知らせしたいことが簡潔に分かるように書かないといけないですね。

Teaching How to Write Documents

 Minamida-sensei, did you write the letter about the year's excursion to send out to the parents?

 Yes. I've done it, but I can't seem to get it right. Can you take a look at it?

 Certainly. Many teachers find it difficult to write correspondence that need to go out to the parents. They don't teach you in school how to write the types of letters that are required after getting a job, nor do they teach you the proper letter formats. Plus, generally there's no need to write such letters in our daily lives, so in the beginning of this job it's common not to be able to write well.

 Especially, I'm not good at using honorific language when writing.

 I can see that. This is pretty bad. Forget the content, to begin with, there are too many typos and omissions. You probably just used the auto correct that came up when you were typing on the computer. Plus, did you even proofread your writing? You're missing periods and you've omitted characters, so parts of what you wrote aren't even words.

When you put your name on these letters and documents, as a homeroom teacher, you're still representing the school. Parents will check the content and use it to judge the entire school. With such poor writing skills, let alone typos and omissions, the parents who receive these letters and documents worry about the standard of the school. It's unfair to lower the image of the school because of your mistakes.

 I am very sorry.

 Furthermore, don't write using colloquial expressions. Of course, it's fine to include direct quotes from a conversation you had with a child. But if you want to write in an indirect form, make sure to replace what you said with the literary form, use conjunctions, and start using a new paragraph whenever you change topics.

You also have too many modifying words. Parents are busy, so say only what needs to be said, and do so in a succinct and easily understood manner, so that reading your letter will be less time consuming.

会話を指導する

南田先生、今、来園された外国人の方になんて聞いてました？

え？何かおかしかったでしょうか？

「Who are you?」と尋ねてませんでしたか？

はい、そうお聞きしました。お名前を聞かないと、メモが残せませんから。

そうじゃないですよ。「Who are you?」ってどういう表現か知っていますか？

「どちら様ですか？」というのは、「Who are you?」で正しいですよね？

違います！「Who are you?」というのは、「あなた、誰？」みたいな気軽に使う英語なんですよ。

え！学校で、「どちら様ですか？」は「Who are you?」と習いました。

お客様にお名前を聞くとき、日本語では、「どちら様ですか？」と丁寧に言うでしょう？英語も同じなんですよ。次からは「May I have your name please?」と聞いてください。ちなみに、電話口で聞くなら「May I ask who's calling please?」と使ってください。

分かりました。すみませんでした。

おっと、その日本語もおかしいですよ。「すみませんでした」と言うのは、相手に謝るときの表現でしょう？あなたは私に悪いことをしたわけではないでしょう？だから、「すみませんでした」ではないですよね。間違えたことを指摘してもらったのだから、感謝の言葉を使うべきですよね。だから、ここでは「アドバイスいただきありがとうございました。」が正しいですね。

なるほど。アドバイスいただき、ありがとうございました。

いえ、どういたしまして。今後は気を付けてくださいね。

日本語にしても、英語にしても言葉って難しいですね。

ほんとですよ！私だって、こうして説明しているけど、いつも言葉使いには悩んでいます。

Teaching about How to Have a Conversation

Minamida-sensei, what did you just ask the foreigner who is visiting?

Why? Did I say something strange?

Didn't you just ask, "Who are you?"

Yes, that's what I said. Without their names, I can't leave a note regarding their visit.

That's not what I'm asking. I would like to know what you think the expression "who are you?" means.

It means, "May I ask who you are?" Right?

No! "Who are you?" in English means "Who are you?"

Really? But I learned in school that, "Who are you?" means, "May I ask who you are?"

In Japanese, you might ask politely, "May I ask your name?", when you ask for the guest's name, right? It's the same with English. Next time, please ask, "May I have your name, please?" If the conversation is over the phone, you can say, "May I ask who's calling, please?"

I understand. I'm sorry.

That's a strange usage, as well. You only need to apologize when you want to express that you're sorry for a mistake you have made. No? In this case you haven't done anything wrong to me, am I right? But, since I pointed out a mistake that you made, shouldn't you rather be thanking me for that? So, in this situation, wouldn't it be correct to say, "Thank you for your advice"?

That's right. And for that, I'll say, "Thank you for your advice."

You're welcome. Just be careful from now on.

Wording is so difficult, whether or not it's in Japanese or English.

I know! I'm still unsure about how to phrase things even when I'm explaining something like this.

有給休暇を使う

園までの通勤が時間的に大変なので、園の近くに引っ越してこようと思います。来月の初めの土曜日に休暇を頂いてよろしいですか？

それは構いません。引っ越し先はもう決めたの？

はい、見つけてあります。

あなたは入園してまだ半年だから、有給休暇は3日だね。

有給休暇を1日使うということでいいかな？

はい、お願いします。

分かりました。それなら、有給休暇の申請書と住宅補助の申請書、交通費変更届け出書を提出してください。

住宅補助が出るということですか？

そのはずです。就業規則を再確認しないと分からないけど、近くに引っ越して来るとなると、毎日支払っている通勤手当が減るわけだから、園としても経費が節約になります。

減額できた範囲の補助はできるはずですよ。ただ、通勤手当は全額非課税だけど、住宅手当は報酬の上乗せとして見られるから、所得が増えることになり、支払う税金は増えるよ。

それでも全額家賃を負担するより少しは助かるはずです。

ありがとうございます。いい制度なので、助かります。就業規則の確認もありがたいです。

転居したら、忘れずに住所変更の届け出書を出してね。住民票の変更もやってね。住所地の市町村民税の納付地も変わるし、選挙権の投票場所も変更になるから、放っておいてはだめだよ。

はい、わかりました。教えていただき、ありがとうございます！

Using Paid Holidays

I'm thinking about moving closer to the school because the commute is too long at the moment. May I take the first Saturday of next month off to move into my new apartment?

That won't be a problem. Have you already decided where you want to move?

Yes, I found a place.

It's only been half a year since you started here, so you have three paid holidays available.

In this case, you will be using one of those paid holidays, is this okay?

Yes, please use that day as one of my paid days off.

Sure. If that's the case, you will need to submit the application forms for paid holidays, housing subsidies, and a notification form for the changes in transportation cost.

Are you saying that I can get my housing subsidized?

I believe so. I need to check with the employment regulations again, but if you move closer to school, the cost of transportation we pay monthly will be reduced, which means for the school, we're saving money on expenses.

Therefore, I'm pretty sure we can subsidize the amount that has been reduced. However, the commuting allowance is tax-exempt for the full amount, but the housing subsidy is seen as extra compensation, so there will be an increase in taxable income that you will have to pay.

Even so, that should still be better than having the burden to pay the full housing fee.

Thank you. This is a very generous policy and I appreciate you looking into the housing regulations again to see if it's, indeed, possible.

Once you move, don't forget to submit a notification for your change of address. Also make sure to change your residency card. The payment location for your district's municipal residential tax will change. Oh, the location for voting will change as well, so you shouldn't leave it until the last minute.

Okay, I understand. Thank you. You have been so helpful!

年間休暇制度

有給休暇制度

当園で６か月以上正社員で勤務をしていた職員は、12日間の有給休暇を取得することができます。１日または半日ごと、別々もしくは連続してとることができます。

職員は、有給休暇申請書（「PLR申請書」）に記入し、園長に提出することにより、いつでも有給休暇を申請することができます。休暇取得の申請日が当園の運営を妨げる場合、園長は別の日に振り替えるよう請うことができます。

産休・育児休業

出産予定の職員は、出産前６週間と出産後８週間の休業を取得することができます。

１歳未満の子を育てる職員は、１年間の育児休業を取得することができます。これは、男性と女性の両方に当てはまります。

代替職員の計画を立てられるよう可能な限り事前に正確な休暇日程を園に知らせてください。また、そのために園長と話し合いをしてください。

介護休業

職員は、以下の場合に休暇を取ることができます。

けがや病気にかかっている子供の世話をする　　　　（子ども一人につき年５回）

病気や障害のある家族の世話をする　　　　　　　　（年３回）

近親者の死去(葬儀の準備など)　　　　　　　　　　（年３回）

やむを得ず欠勤する場合は、代替職員の手配が必要となりますので、
可能な限り事前に園に知らせてください。

ABC

Annual Paid Leave

Annual Paid Leave

Every staff member at Fore Garden Preschool who has worked full time for more than six months is entitled to twelve days of paid leave. These may be taken separately or consecutively, in increments of a full day or half-day.

Staff members may request a day of paid leave at any time by filling out the Paid Leave Request Form ("PLR Form") and submitting it to the Principal. If the requested day greatly interferes with the operation of the school, the Principal may ask the staff member to choose a different day instead.

Maternity, Paternity and Child Care Leave

Any Fore Garden Preschool employee who is expecting a child may take six weeks of leave before childbirth and eight weeks after childbirth. Those

Any Fore Garden Preschool employee may take up to one year of leave to watch a child who is less than one year old. This applies to both men and women.

Fore Garden Preschool kindly asks that expecting parents inform the school about their exact dates of leave as far in advance as possible so that we can make plans for a substitute teacher during that time period. Please schedule a meeting with the principal to discuss this information.

Family Care Leave

Fore Garden Preschool employees are entitled to take leave under the following circumstances:

To care for a child who has injury or illness   (5 days/child)

To care for a family member who is ill or disabled   (3 days/year)

To deal with the death of a family member (care, funeral arrangements, etc.)
                                                                (3 days/year)

Once again, please do you best to inform the school in advance of all absences so we can make arrangements for a replacement.

インフォメーション

検定内容・申込に関するご案内

検定日、級別レベル、出題範囲、受検方法、受検料、支払い方法など本検定に関する
情報及び受検申込みについては、不定期に変更・追加となるため、本書ではご案内を
掲載しておりません。
詳細については当協会幼保ホームページ https://www.youhoeigo.com
でご確認ください。

幼保英語検定

教材のご紹介とご案内

本検定向けの各種学習教材は、㈱ブックフォレより出版、販売を行っております。
当協会からの直接の購入はできません。各種学習教材に関しては、
出版元の (株) ブックフォレよりご案内、ご紹介をしております。
㈱ブックフォレのホームページ https://bookfore.co.jpでご確認ください。

㈱ブックフォレ

オンライン学習ツールのご案内

単語学習につきましては、㈱mikanの専用アプリをご活用ください。

App Store: 「英単語アプリ mikan」をApp Storeで (apple.com)
Google Play: 【mikan】幼保英語検定単語帳アプリ

App Store

オンライン授業用ツール及び自宅学習用ツールとしてオンデマンド講座を開講しています。
オンデマンド講座に関する詳しい内容は、主催一般社団法人国際子育て人材支
援機構(OBP) ホームページ www.obp.academyをご覧ください。

Google Play

OBP

資格カードの発行について

検定合格後、合格証以外にご希望の方には合格を証明する幼保英語士資格証を
発行しています。カード形式で携帯がすることができ、身分証明書としての利用も
可能です。資格証申請方法など詳しくは 幼保ホームページをご覧ください。

資格証について

幼保英語を活かした活躍について

国内及び海外での活躍の場を国際子育て人材エージェンシーでご相談を受付けて
おります。
詳細につきましては、同社ホームページ http://www.obpjob.comをご覧ください。

OBP JOB

TAIP 推薦状

The Tokyo Association of International Preschools (TAIP) is a group of preschools that work together to bring professional development events and publicity to the international early childhood education community in Japan. Our organization continues to evolve with each passing year, bringing both traditional and forward-thinking methods of learning and promotion to all our members.

The organization was founded in 2005 under the motto "Preschool for Preschoolers," and now includes dozens of schools of all shapes and sizes. Many are in the greater Kanto area but others are farther away, as we continue to grow to help early childhood educators throughout Japan.

TAIP strongly supports the work of Youho Eigo Kentei as a valuable contribution to the future of Japanese education and to Japanese society at large. We will continue to back their efforts in the future.

Moving forward we will carefully consider the needs of our international members as their relevance continues to grow within the Japanese early childhood education community.

We encourage you to check our website (https://www.tokyopreschools.org/) for more information, including membership options and upcoming events.

Tokyo Association of International Preschools Board of Directors

TAIP Homepage

幼児教育・保育英語検定　1級テキスト

2021年12月22日第二版第1刷

著　者　　一般社団法人　幼児教育・保育英語検定協会

発行所　　一般社団法人　幼児教育・保育英語検定協会
　　　　　〒153-0061　東京都目黒区中目黒3-6-2
　　　　　TEL 03-5725-3224　FAX 03-6452-4148　https://www.youhoeigo.com

発売所　　BOOKFORE　株式会社　ブックフォレ
　　　　　〒224-0003　神奈川県横浜市都筑区中川中央1-21-3-2F
　　　　　TEL 045-910-1020　FAX 045-910-1040
　　　　　http://www.bookfore.co.jp

印刷・製本　　冊子印刷社

© 2020, Organization of Test of English for Teachers　　Printed in Japan
ISBN : 978-4-909846-47-1